Praise for *Repotting*

*"**Repotting: 10 Steps for Redesigning Your Life** is an essential tool for all women who want to jump-start a new life, including breast-cancer survivors."*

— Honorable **Nancy G. Brinker**, former ambassador to Hungary and breast-cancer advocate

*"As a woman who has repotted many times, I highly recommend **Repotting: 10 Steps for Redesigning Your Life**. I wish I'd had this book to help me with my own repotting journey on the way to becoming a member of Congress."*

— Honorable **Ellen Tauscher**, U.S. House of Representatives, 10th District of California

"For every woman who is searching for a more meaningful life, this is <u>the book</u>—a how-to handbook for 21st-century repotters. Don't leave home without it!"

— **Chris Boskin**, retired magazine publisher; board member of *Yoga Journal* magazine

Repotting

Hay House Titles of Related Interest

Being in Balance: *9 Principles for Creating Habits to Match Your Desires,* by Dr. Wayne W. Dyer

Everything I've Ever Done That Worked, by Lesley Garner

Four Acts of Personal Power: *How to Heal Your Past and Create a Positive Future,* by Denise Linn

Inner Peace for Busy Women: *Balancing Work, Family, and Your Inner Life,* by Joan Z. Borysenko, Ph.D.

Life Is Short—Wear Your Party Pants, by Loretta LaRoche

The Power of Infinite Love and Gratitude: *An Evolutionary Journey to Awakening Your Spirit,* by Dr. Darren R. Weissman

Yes, You Can Get a Financial Life!: *Your Lifetime Guide to Financial Planning,* by Ben Stein and Phil DeMuth

You Can Heal Your Life, by Louise L. Hay

All of the above are available at your
local bookstore, or may be ordered by visiting:

Hay House USA: **www.hayhouse.com**®
Hay House Australia: **www.hayhouse.com.au**
Hay House UK: **www.hayhouse.co.uk**
Hay House South Africa: **orders@psdprom.co.za**
Hay House India: **www.hayhouseindia.co.in**

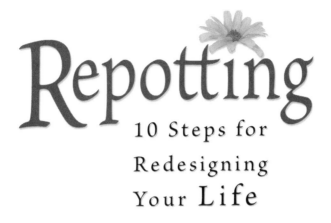

Repotting

10 Steps for
Redesigning
Your Life

DIANA HOLMAN AND GINGER PAPE

HAY HOUSE, INC.
Carlsbad, California
London • Sydney • Johannesburg
Vancouver • Hong Kong • New Delhi

Published and distributed in the United States by: Hay House, Inc.: www.hayhouse.com • *Published and distributed in Australia by:* Hay House Australia Pty. Ltd.: www.hayhouse.com.au • *Published and distributed in the United Kingdom by:* Hay House UK, Ltd.: www.hayhouse.co.uk • *Published and distributed in the Republic of South Africa by:* Hay House SA (Pty), Ltd.: orders@psdprom.co.za • *Distributed in Canada by:* Raincoast: www.raincoast.com • *Published in India by:* Hay House Publishers India: www.hayhouseindia.co.in

Editorial supervision: Jill Kramer • *Design:* Tricia Breidenthal

Library of Congress Cataloging-in-Publication Data

Holman, Diana.
  Repotting : 10 steps for redesigning your life / Diana Holman and Ginger Pape. -- 1st ed.
    p. cm.
  Includes bibliographical references.
  ISBN-13: 978-1-4019-1146-1 (hardcover)
  ISBN-13: 978-1-4019-1147-8 (tradepaper) 1. Self-actualization (Psychology) 2. Women--Conduct of life. 3. Quality of life. I. Pape, Ginger. II. Title.
  BF637.S4H62 2007
  158.1--dc22

                                                        2006028653

Hardcover ISBN 13: 978-1-4019-1146-1
Tradepaper ISBN 13: 978-1-4019-1147-8

10 09 08 07   4 3 2 1
1st edition, March 2007

Printed in the United States of America

To our daughters,
Hilary and Sarah;
our granddaughters;
and all women reporters,
current and future.

Contents

Foreword

When my girlfriends Ginger and Diana first told me their concept for this book, I was so excited! You wouldn't believe how many times I've repotted myself. What I didn't realize is that this happened because I needed a new pot—a new life—and room for personal growth. I thought there was something wrong with me and was feeling frustrated and unfulfilled. It was as if I were flying blind—I couldn't see the way to fulfillment.

So I rethought my direction and made changes. Now, as I look back on my life, it's easy to see. There was *nothing* wrong with me; I was just repotting. I was doing what I was supposed to—continuing to grow as a person. My old situation was just too small to contain my vision. Think about it: What happens to a beautiful, flowering plant that outgrows its container? If you don't repot it, it eventually withers and dies.

Since the *Wonder Woman* series ended, I've lived a life of multiple identities—wife, mother, singer, spokesperson for a variety of products and causes, and, of course, actress. When I read this book, I felt an immediate connection and recognized my own journey in the stories of other women. I've had to make many of the same choices as the repotters you'll read about. My journey to find self-fulfillment has led me to put my personal values and priorities in focus: I now have a wonderful family *and* an acting career.

For those of you who want to change your lives, this is an essential handbook. Even Wonder Woman could have benefited from its ideas and step-by-step approach. Considering the fast pace you're probably maintaining today, this book will make you pause, take stock of where you are now and where you want to go, and help you create a workable plan to redesign your life.

As anyone who has ever planted and tended a garden knows, it's a work in progress. There are successes and failures; and sometimes you need to uproot a plant, a bed, or an entire yard in order to make it grow. If women want to flourish, we need to repot, too. And even if we don't reach our original goals, the journey is worthwhile in and of itself!

— **Lynda Carter**

Preface

We're at a watershed moment in history. Across the country, women of all ages are embracing a new mind-set as they rewrite their journeys, often multiple times, to bring their values and passions to the forefront. We've tracked this phenomenon in the past 30 years in our careers as trend experts, entrepreneurs, and corporate executives. We've watched as this metamorphosis has grown into a movement in which women of all ages and life stages are now participating. We decided to write this book to capture this transformational moment and provide a handbook to help others on this path.

In recent years, much attention has been given to the subject of women's reinvention and search to connect with their inner passions. Our goal was to take a fresh look at this subject and introduce a new vocabulary for it. "Repotting" is a metaphor for the creative process that women must undertake in order to develop themselves as they search for a more meaningful life. Gardeners who want to move plants to a new environment to promote growth need to create a base plan with steps to design a well-organized garden. In the same way, those who are embarking on a journey to redesign their lives need a master landscape plan incorporating certain steps that will provide the framework for their new lives.

From our research and experience, we know that women need more than generalizations to guide them as they initiate their search for a new identity. Repotting is not a "one size fits all" process, and every woman's experience is unique. The step-by-step, interactive exercises we've created will allow you to develop your own personalized approach to redesigning your life.

We recognize that making any change—but particularly one involving a life redesign—can be daunting. Our goal is to show you how to overcome any hesitation you might feel by providing you with a concrete, accessible, reader-friendly "how to" guide. Each chapter contains exercises that will help you identify your passions, evaluate your own situation, and anticipate any obstacles so that you can create a workable, flexible plan tailored to your needs.

While the two of us have created new identities for ourselves throughout our adult lives and have learned from those experiences, we're aware that there's a whole world of women repotters whose stories are waiting to be told. In our professional roles, we've conducted focus groups and other types of research on those who are revamping their lives, as well as counseled individuals from all walks of life on how to successfully reinvent themselves.

When we began to write this book and tell those stories, we decided to add to our research base by interviewing women who were in various stages of the repotting process in the new millennium. In these conversations, we encountered a "no boundaries" mind-set that is one of the most significant and inspirational aspects of the repotting trend.

Every chapter of this book incorporates lessons learned from real-life women who are engaged in repotting. We think you'll find that their willingness to change despite obstacles, and the stories of how they made those shifts, are both inspirational and instructional. We hope that you'll view these repotters as role models. (Please note that in many cases, we've changed the names of the repotting interviewees we've profiled at their request. Some of the profiles are composites of several interviewees.)

We feel that the combination of the repotting lexicon, the interactive exercises, and the real-life examples make this book uniquely useful. We hope that you will enjoy reading it as much as we enjoyed writing it. As we sat at the kitchen table crafting each chapter, we found ourselves caught up in the lives of so many wonderful women. This book is a celebration of them, and of all who want to join the repotting movement.

Repotting

by Gunilla Norris

How hard it is to know
when the pot is too small for the plant.
Some plants need to be contained, held very close.
Others cannot be crowded.
I don't know when I myself am too pot-bound,
lacking courage to be replanted,
to take the shock of new soil, to feel into the unknown and
to take root in it.

This drying out, this self-crowding
sneaks up on me. It seems I must always feel
a little wilted or deadened before I know
I am too pot-bound.

This african violet must first be cut
and divided. The knife goes through the root.
The white flesh exposed and moist
looks as if it is bleeding.
It must have soil immediately
so the plant won't die.
Then water. Water taken in from below.
This water must seep up into the plant
by infusion. Then comes the waiting
as the shock registers.
Days and weeks of waiting.

It will be months before a new leaf appears.
Perhaps the plant won't make it.
So it is when the time comes for me to be cut
and divided so as to grow again.

Help me to see this not as a problem
but as a process. Help me to surrender
to the growth that only comes with pain,
with division, with helplessness, with waiting.
Especially the days and weeks of waiting.

From *Being Home: A Book of Meditations*

Introduction

Becoming a New You

It's a cold and dreary winter day, and you're looking out your window at the bare trees. You sense that in a blink of an eye, the season will begin to turn into spring, and this gray landscape will change. Growth and color will be evident all around—budding branches will appear on trees, bulbs will sprout up through the earth, yellow daffodils and forsythias will dot the ground, and a hint of green grass will catch your eye. Suddenly, a landscape that was barren and dull will become full of the promise of new possibilities—for rebirth, rejuvenation, and redirection.

Spring is a period of renewal. For gardeners, it's a time to look at their landscape and make design decisions—to make additions, reseed, or repot plants that have been languishing in places that aren't quite right for them. The *New York Times* obituary of Christopher Lloyd, the renowned gardener and author, reported that he said, "Your garden should not be frozen in time—it shouldn't become a museum."

Like the natural world, your life is dynamic and ever changing; you're capable of transformation and growth, too. How you design your personal landscape is based upon your own set of values, which have to be lived and felt. You're your own landscape architect, and as you undertake your life-design process, recognize that you're creating a future for yourself.

Many women, from movie stars to your next-door neighbor, are reworking their personal gardens right now. Celebrities such as Danielle Steel, Madonna, Donna Karan, and Elizabeth Hurley are finding new ways to express themselves. You probably have a friend who's reinventing herself—perhaps starting on a more fulfilling career or volunteering for a new cause. Maybe you, too, are already repotting.

In gardening, the term *repot* means to move a plant from its current container or flower bed when it needs new conditions in order to flourish. You may be finding yourself in the same state as a cramped and root-bound begonia. As you examine and reevaluate things, you may be asking yourself: *Is it time to repot myself and grow in a new environment? Is it time to add more meaning to my life? Is it time to redesign my personal landscape?*

Whatever stage you've reached, you're not alone. Congratulations are in order! You're part of a movement—the repotting movement—whose members are all around you. Whether you're at a PTA meeting, a cocktail party, or the health club, you're bound to meet women who are either going through the repotting process themselves or know someone who is. She may be a corporate executive who left the fast track to start a family and later became an "inventor mom," or she could be a woman in her 80s who, after careers as a nurse, scientist, and sculptor, decided to launch a nonprofit organization devoted to providing art classes for elderly Alzheimer's patients. Many breast-cancer patients and survivors are repotters, focusing on aligning their outer worlds with their core values. This metamorphosis process is happening to women every minute of each and every day.

Overcoming the Fear Factor

Make no mistake: Repotting takes a lot of work. As one woman said, "This repotting thing isn't easy. This isn't paint by the numbers. We have no road maps and no paths to follow—we have to make our own way." Most of those we interviewed for this book experienced some difficulty in their transition. Many are caught between the needs of others and their own; some are sandwiched between children and aging parents. Others perceive a conflict between their personal obligations and their professional ambitions. All of them agreed that a successful repotter needs to have a combination of discipline, honesty with herself, and courage in order to successfully undergo the repotting process.

Many of us are challenged by our own fears. When we're about to begin repotting, we have to face the fear factor associated with risk taking. Changing our lifestyle or choosing a new career or set of priorities can make us feel vulnerable and uncertain. The challenge of learning something new as we age is also often a primary deterrent to reinvention. Whether we're repotting ourselves or a seedling, our concern is the same: Will the transplant succeed? Will it flourish?

For many women, the choice between the comfortable but unfulfilling status quo and an unknown future creates enormous fear. This may be related to finances, such as a potential drop in income resulting from giving up a high-powered but unsatisfying job. Or it could be anxiety over letting go, such as being afraid to leave a mediocre job because they can't be sure they'll do better somewhere else. If women haven't been working, the thought of testing themselves—as volunteers, in new positions, or whatever—may be daunting. In short, a variety of cultural, financial, or family-related obstacles may create barriers for repotters.

About This Book

This book is divided into two parts for easy use. Part I is designed to help you decide if you're ready, willing, or able to repot, with Chapter 1 providing many tools to assist you in beginning this process. In Chapters 2 through 5, we'll help you focus on key issues in your life, including:

- **Time:** Analyze, manage, and maximize it. Discover how to prune your activities and weed out what's no longer useful or relevant to create more space in your life for what you really want to do. (See Chapter 2: "Do You Need More Space Around You?")

- **Health:** Take the necessary steps to nourish your body, mind, and soul. (See Chapter 3: "Do You Need More Light?")

- **Lifelong learning:** Fertilize your life with all kinds of educational pursuits that will foster the growth of the seeds you plant. (See Chapter 4: "Do You Need More Fertilizer?")

- **Risk taking:** Understand the risks involved in transplanting yourself into a new environment. (See Chapter 5: "Have You Outgrown Your Current Planter?")

Part II will teach you how to develop a personal landscape plan using various exercises. Chapters 6 through 10 will focus on:

- **Changing seasons:** Recognizing the touchstones in your personal garden. (See Chapter 6: "Identifying Your Personal Touchstone")

- **Digging into your landscape:** Doing the necessary research for successful repotting. (See Chapter 7: "Repotting Research: Digging into Your Garden")

- **Partial repotting:** Addressing one area at a time—not everyone can or wants to undertake a total redesign of her life. (See Chapter 8: "Partial Repotting: Cultivating One Flower Bed at a Time")

- **Transplanting yourself:** Creating a customized repotting plan. (See Chapter 9: "Cultivating a New Life and Transplanting Successfully")

Finally, you'll find **Rules for Repotting** in Chapter 10, plus resource lists that can be used as reference guides for you.

Personal Gardening Tip: Do the spadework. You'll need to till your own garden—in other words, get underneath the topsoil to find your own answers to each and every exercise in this book—in order to create both a "mindscape" and a landscape design that will equip you to become a "new you."

Equipment for Repotters

As you read this book, you'll need repotting equipment or materials. To help you get started, we've developed the *Repotting 101 Workbook*. You can download this workbook from our Website, **www.repotting.com**. This workbook contains:

- Preprinted exercises from this book

- Formatted pages to create both your Personal Garden Calendar (PGC) and a *revised* Personal Garden Calendar (described on page xxv)

- The Values Orbit diagram and exercise from Chapter 6

- Personal Gardening Tips from Chapters 1 through 9

- Space for notes and ideas that occur to you on your repotting journey

- A summary of the rules for repotting for handy reference

Once you've downloaded the complete document and placed it in a binder or folder, you'll want to carry it with you at all times to help keep you organized and focused on your repotting journey.

If you prefer to create your own materials, you'll need:

- Repotting notebooks (we recommend a three-ring binder and a small portable one) in which you'll keep track of the exercises in this book

- Blank paper to create your Personal Garden Calendar and a revised Personal Garden Calendar and pages to jot down notes on your ideas

- File folders for organizing your repotting research and miscellaneous materials that you gather during your repotting journey.

Personal Gardening Tip: Start from day one to gather and organize all materials that relate to and could potentially help you think about, plan, and carry out your repotting program.

Repotting Notebooks

Since repotting is a creative process, the first thing you'll need is your imagination. To keep track of any and all of your thoughts, you'll need either the *Repotting*

101 Workbook you've downloaded or a notebook you've purchased on your own. Pick something you like that's portable. Creativity isn't restricted to a time or place, so you'll want something that can go wherever you do, in your car or handbag—to work, to a playgroup, to school, or on a walk with your dog. It should even be on your bedside table, as many women have their best thoughts when it's quiet and the lights are out.

Repotting Files

In addition to our workbook or your notebook(s), you'll need several file folders. As we said, repotting is a cumulative process, and you'll be adding materials along the way. In the appropriate section of our workbook or in a file folder labeled "Exercises," keep copies of all the exercises that you'll be asked to do in the upcoming chapters. For example, in Chapter 6 you'll be creating your **Values Orbit**, a diagram that you'll need to refer to often, which is contained in our workbook, or which you'll create and put in your own system.

In another file—called the **Idea File**—keep all the information that you'll find from outside sources: articles you've clipped, Internet research, and other notes you make that are relevant to your repotting journey. For instance, during the **Think Week** described in Chapter 7, you'll be gathering additional materials from a wide variety of places. It's critical that you keep all your materials organized and in an easily accessible place from the start.

Other files may be used for organizing information on a passion you choose to pursue as you repot. For instance, if your goal is to start a new business, you'll need your timeline and related tasks together in one place (see the **Landscape Master Plan** in the Appendix). Or you may collect articles on a hobby, such as photography or knitting. Develop a filing system that works for you.

Personal Garden Calendar

The most essential tool you'll create and use is your **Personal Garden Calendar** (PGC), a must-have tool for you to use throughout the book. You'll learn how to create the PGC in Chapter 1 because it's the key to understanding, initiating, organizing, and launching your journey. Repotting 101—the curriculum for new repotters—requires more than shuffling a "Life at a Glance" page in a Day-Timer planner.

The *Repotting 101 Workbook*, available on **www.repot ting.com**, contains a formatted Personal Garden Calendar and a *revised* Personal Garden Calendar for your use. If you aren't using our workbook, we'll tell you in Chapter 1 how to create your PGC, which will show your current schedule and, more important, make room for revisions as you envision your new life.

Once you've completed the exercises in the first two chapters, you'll need to make notes and revisions on your PGC about how you're currently spending your time. Ultimately, you'll use the revised PGC in the workbook or create your own in order to provide a framework for the exercises throughout the rest of this book. Keep this handy—you'll need to refer to it frequently.

Create Space for Personal Gardening Tips

At the end of each chapter, we've provided key ideas about what you've read—**Personal Gardening Tips.** Because these serve as useful repotting reminders, you may want to write them on sticky notes and place them on a wall or some other surface, wherever you want to be reminded of these little nuggets. These tips are also summarized for easy reference in the *Repotting 101 Workbook.*

Authors as Repotters

Both of us are experienced repotters who have reinvented ourselves many times. Diana started work as a teacher in the Middle East and became a fashion consultant in Europe. After lobbying and working for the government in Washington, D.C., she realized that she wanted to be out from under the proverbial "glass ceiling." Her strong desire to test her own limits and find a lifestyle-friendly career led her to start and run not just one, but two, companies. Her interest in women's lifestyle issues led her to create WomanTrend, a company dedicated to tracking and interpreting trends created by and impacting women. After overcoming her initial fears about income, success, and family issues, Diana never looked back.

After 20 years, the constant travel and demands of entrepreneurship took their toll. When her granddaughter asked, "Why did you miss my school play?" Diana knew it was time to reprioritize and place family and a new lifestyle first. Today, Diana consults with clients on a schedule that suits her values and varied interests.

Ginger also started work as a teacher, first in Massachusetts, then moving to Washington, D.C., where she ultimately became a lobbyist. After ten years, Ginger wanted to learn something entirely different. She moved to New York City to work as an executive on Wall Street. When she married her husband, who lived in Washington, D.C., Ginger moved back and opened an office for the American Stock Exchange. This move allowed her to combine her Wall Street work with her lobbying skills.

It was Lillian Vernon, board member of the American Stock Exchange, who helped Ginger overcome the fear factor associated with starting her own business. Noting that 50 percent of the battle is overcoming such reservations, Lillian told her to take the plunge and become an entrepreneur—and Ginger did just that. In this chapter of her life, she was an early adopter of job sharing, flexible hours, and additional techniques that allowed her and other working women to combine family and work.

When Ginger's husband took on a more demanding job, she rethought her situation and sold her business. Ginger cofounded the Women's Business Center (WBC) to help women from all backgrounds have access to entrepreneurial training to enable them to start their own businesses. She also helped found the Washington "Race for the Cure" for the Susan G. Komen Breast Cancer Foundation. For the last 15 years, she has consulted with women from all walks of life on their repotting process. She has also participated in varied community-based projects and focuses on her family.

Our two stories share many of the same elements as those of the hundreds of women we've interviewed. Some of these elements include: a strong desire to make positive changes in our lives, a willingness to face all the challenges associated with such changes, and a recognition that finding a new identity is an ongoing work in progress. All of us want the same thing: to fulfill ourselves and be the best we can be while living a life that works.

Your Repotting Journey

Your motivation to embark on a repotting journey may be similar to that of our interviewees or it may be totally different. Whatever the case, you'll find useful lessons and inspiration to take with you from this book. Think of it as a guide to creating your personal landscape plan, but remember: *You* have to decide which plants go where. No one else can—or should—do it for you.

Just as creating a new garden is a work in progress, so, too, is redesigning your life. Your vision for both may be affected along the way by unforeseen events. But no matter what happens, the journey itself is worth pursuing. Research shows that happiness is linked as much to the anticipation of a new or different outcome as it is to the final result. The process of repotting itself will bring you a greater sense of well-being and meaning in your life.

ARE YOU READY TO REPOT?

A Repotting Mix: The Variety Pack

There's never been a better time than now to embark on the process of repotting. Thousands—maybe millions—of women have decided that this is the season for change, and they realize that they're responsible for making the decision to repot. They're moving *choice* to the top of their list and are defining what works for them; they're shedding old notions, others' expectations, and outmoded concepts in favor of a personalized approach to life. If you're tempted to redesign your landscape but haven't acted on your feelings yet, we hope that you'll be encouraged to join the repotting movement.

If you're reading this book, then you've probably reached the point in your life where you want to listen to your heart, not your head, and join a growing number of women who are redesigning their lives. If you haven't begun the change yet, but want to, this book will inspire you with stories about women who have reshaped their lives and validate your own journey toward personal metamorphosis. If you've already begun, the interactive exercises may confirm your decision-making process, or they may bring up alternative ways of looking at your situation and foster new ideas.

Types of Repotters

As trend spotters and experts on entrepreneurial endeavors, we've witnessed the seeds of change for 21st-century women. In our own research, involving hundreds of women across the country, some of whom are profiled in this book, we confirmed that the repotting movement is in full bloom. And just as every garden contains a mix of plants, we found many types of repotters in this growing movement.

- **On-the-verge repotters.** Some women are in a quandary. They have a feeling that things aren't quite right, but they don't have the tools to create a new landscape plan for themselves.

- **Change-point repotters.** A dramatic event has motivated these women to change the plan for their life landscape. They need to face the interruption in the status quo, deal with the emotions and realities of the experience, and assess how it impacts them. Their challenge is to create a new strategy incorporating their transformation.

- **Core repotters.** These individuals often go full circle to find their authentic selves. They may return to a touchstone of their youth or uncover an interest they'd put aside because of their life's circumstances. Women may strip away years of activities that clutter their landscape in order to get back in touch with the essence of who they are or who they want to be.

- **Values repotters.** These women are reassessing their lives in the context of changing priorities. Their "Values Orbits," which we discuss in Chapter 6, encompass everything from health to education, finance, and relationships. As life goes on, all women face new circumstances that require them to reprioritize and reassess their values system. A search for fulfillment is a centerpiece for many.

- **Spiritual repotters.** In spite of the rewards of career advancement, academic accomplishments, and achievements in a multitude of other areas, many women still feel something is missing in their lives. Their repotting process often involves a search to fill this empty core, especially finding ways to give back.

- **Extreme-makeover repotters.** For some, redesigning their lives means a radical departure from their current existence. They may choose to jump off a cliff into the unknown because challenge motivates them and brings them fulfillment.

- **Serial repotters.** Just as your garden goes through continual renewal, so can you. There's no limit to the number of times you can repot yourself. Every season offers opportunities for new growth, and what's fulfilling to you now may not answer your needs in a future stage of life.

If you're on the verge of becoming a repotter or are in transition from an old identity to a new one, Part I of our book will be especially helpful. It's designed to assist you in determining if you're ready to repot, and if so, what tools you'll need to launch the process. Chapters 1 through 5 will take you through a step-by-step review of your current lifestyle and how to create the right environment for this change.

You may not feel ready to undertake a major overhaul of your personal garden. It may not be appropriate to strip out everything in sight, including the trees. You may have to start small—weeding a bed, planting a few seeds, or just pruning existing plants. Of course, you may face unexpected events or detours along the way, but don't let that deter you. Give yourself permission to take the risk, because pursuing change—with its inspiration, stimulation, and potential for growth—can be a reward in itself.

Chapter One

How Do You Know You're Ready?

It's Monday morning, and Gwen is organizing her brief-case to head off to the law firm where she works. After a weekend of nonstop motion during which she managed her children's activities, her home, and her social life, Gwen is just about to launch into the new week. As she's going through some papers on her overloaded desk at home, a sealed envelope appears. She opens it, only to find an invitation to a cocktail party at the home of the senior partner in her law firm. The problem? The event took place two days ago. Now she's embarrassed to go to work and wonders what else is lurking on her desk that needs attention. But she's already ten minutes late and doesn't have time to excavate the piles.

Kimberly, a vice president of sales for a major pharmaceutical firm, travels constantly and is in the process of moving from a one-bedroom condominium to her first town house. She's looking forward to developing a broader community of friends and a better social life in her new setting and hopes to meet someone she'd like to marry and, eventually, start a family. At the moment, however, her demanding career continues to dominate her life.

As she packs for her next business trip, Kimberly realizes that her closet is full of winter clothes—and it's now spring. The problem? She doesn't have time to search for a lightweight suit and ends up packing a wool one, even though the weather forecast predicts that the temperature will reach 70 degrees. She's had no free time and won't in the foreseeable future, so she's had no chance to sort out her closet, update her wardrobe for the new season, or meet her social goals.

Julia takes pride in being involved in the lives of her three children. Having given up her job to raise a family, she puts her considerable energy and organizational skills into managing her home. When she quit her job, she anticipated having pockets of free time but has overloaded herself. Her days are filled with school volunteer events, ferrying children to and from activities, and a host of community-related pursuits. The problem? Julia's schedule is so packed that last week she showed up on the wrong day for her daughter's gymnastics show. Her little girl feels hurt because this isn't the first time her mother has missed an important event—and it probably won't be the last.

Susan recently retired from her job as a consultant for an executive search firm, and her children are grown with families of their own. She and her husband anticipated retiring at the same time, but because his company has launched a new venture with him in charge, he's working even longer hours. In the first six months of her retirement, Susan found many ways to fill her day: fitness classes, bridge lessons, recording for the blind, and a whole raft of unfocused activities. The problem? At the end of the day, she wonders where the time has gone and realizes that she still hasn't opened the day's mail or phoned the travel agent to plan a trip with her husband. In the back of her mind, Susan wonders where her sense of purpose has gone.

These stories are snapshots of new-millennium women who are living such fast-forward lives that they lack the time or focus to reflect on and identify what's meaningful to them. Accomplished, competent women such as Gwen, Kimberly, Julia, and Susan all suffer from symptoms of overload. They have type A lives, and at the end of the day, they feel a gnawing sense of incompleteness.

With their time filled with details and to-do lists, many women today are discovering that they haven't found the time to focus on themselves and what's important to them. As this "spin cycle" life goes on for days, weeks, and even months, they're wrestling with questions such as these:

- Is what I'm doing meaningful to me?

- Is it time for me to reach out beyond my immediate family to help others in the world around me?

- Should I reallocate my tasks so that I can spend more time in endeavors that renew my spirit?

If you're asking yourself these questions, maybe it's time for you to repot.

What Is Repotting?

What does redesigning your life have to do with gardening, repotting plants, and designing landscapes? It doesn't matter whether you're one of the more than 57 million female gardeners in the United States (according to the U.S. Census Bureau) or you've never held a spade in your life. The horticultural metaphors employed throughout this book will help you understand the elements of your own life and how you can replant yourself to become a new you.

Let's look more closely at what gardening entails. A garden is a work in progress that's affected by a wide variety of elements, including climate, weather, soil, water, sun, and shade. The composition of your garden plot is also a matter of choice and subject to change over time. At first you may plant shrubs, annuals, and grasses. At another point in time, you may change your plan and add vines, trees, and perennials. As the landscape architect, you're in charge of design and maintenance: tilling the soil, fertilizing, planting, pruning, weeding, and watering.

This is true in your life as well, which, like a garden, is dynamic and ever changing. To redesign your personal landscape, you have to analyze all the elements in it, then visualize your ideal existence and develop a master plan. And if you're reading this book, you probably *do* want to change your current environment. Whether you'd like to make wholesale changes (redoing entire vistas) or simply alter one aspect (replanting a flower bed), you'll need to undertake a step-by-step design process.

Making your master plan involves considering a number of elements, and in the coming chapters we'll help you analyze all of them. Like a landscape architect, you'll need to undertake the following steps:

1. **Conduct a survey.** Just as a gardener does a complete survey of the area to be planted, you need to take stock of your current life. We'll help you look at whether the choices you're

thinking of making accurately reflect your values and circumstances.

2. **Take an inventory.** Gardeners take note of all the elements that affect their landscape. We'll help you review all the components of your life that will influence your decision making, including family, job, financial needs, health, and other key motivating factors.

3. **Create a base plan.** After a landscape designer has done a survey and inventory of the fundamental elements in the garden, she develops a base plan for the redesign. We'll help you examine all the essentials in your current life and decide what you want to take with you, what you want to weed out, and what new essentials you want to add to your redesigned life.

4. **Prepare a flexible program.** Gardeners need to look at a variety of options and develop alternatives in order to accommodate all the possibilities. We'll show you how to formulate your own program to redesign your life. This will involve looking at many options in addition to your main goal. A critical part of the planning process is to prepare yourself for the inevitable droughts, freezes, and weeds you'll encounter. The repotting process will only be successful if you're prepared to "blossom where you're planted"—in other words, if you can be flexible enough to make the most of your situation, whatever it is.

5. **Review your final design.** Only after you've confirmed that you're satisfied with all the information you've gathered in each of the design-process steps will you be ready to move forward. Putting plants into your garden—implementing your redesigned life landscape plan—is the last step. You'll never understand how the color, texture, shape, and spacing of the plants will mesh unless you have an overall framework. We hope that by the time you've finished this book, you'll have a better understanding of how you can repot your life.

A Repotter's Story

Our friend Chris embodies the word *repotter*. For a long time, she lived a spin-cycle life, spending years as an executive building a successful career in the world of publishing. Her frenzied schedule and overloaded days were sapping her vitality. She moved from being an editor at a major magazine to becoming the publisher and cofounder of another magazine, and her professional life was a continual upward climb. Family-health issues, a desire to spend more time with her husband, an inability to pursue her passion for yoga, and her desire for a less hectic life led Chris to push the pause button. A confirmed gardener, she decided to do to herself what she did to her plants: repot. She needed to transplant herself into a more healthful environment.

As Chris has said, this didn't happen overnight. She was determined to work forever but admits that she felt unsettled. You could say that she was wilting under the pressure of too many meetings and her own increasing sense of unease. It took her three years to face her feelings and map out a new landscape design for her life.

Chris struggled with a number of questions, including:

- Who am I if I don't have a title?

- Am I willing to give up a regular paycheck?

- How do I want to spend the major part of my day—in an office or outside?

- What's important to me and how do I translate that into my everyday life?

- Am I devoting enough time to my husband and other family members?

- Do I need to reinvent who I am and how I live?

- How much more time do I need to take care of myself?

- At this point in my life, am I doing what's really meaningful to me?

Your own sense that you're ready to repot may come gradually, as Chris's did, or you may have an "Aha!" moment that suddenly clarifies that you must make a change. It could be when your husband says, "It's been three months since we've had an evening for just the two of us. How do I get on your agenda?" Perhaps it's when your boss, knowing you're sick, says that he still expects you to come into work on the weekend. Or maybe it's when you look in the mirror at the end of the day and you almost don't recognize the person you see because you have no vitality, you're unhappy, and you feel drained. For working women with children, it's often the moment when a child says, "Are you ever going to be home to put me to bed?"

It's All About Time

The challenge for most women is finding enough time. Much has been written about this topic and the trends surrounding it, including the effect of technology on both expanding and compressing women's lives: The more time-saving devices we have, the more tasks we try to squeeze into our days. The crunch is reflected in such lifestyle choices as taking children along on business trips in order to see them more often (a growing trend) or having take-out meals instead of cooking. Whether you're in a demanding job or managing a family at home, lack of time may be a concern and even a constant pressure. Becoming aware of how you actually spend your days versus how you want to is the first step in developing a realistic repotting plan. The exercises in this chapter are designed to help you analyze and address the time concerns in your life.

Eileen's Story: The "Lightbulb" Moment

One of the women we interviewed, Eileen, had a lightbulb moment when her youngest daughter (then five years old) asked, "Are you ever going to be home to have dinner with me?" Eileen was a television news correspondent who'd been working 24/7 reporting on the crisis of September 11, 2001. This event heightened her awareness of her desire to be with her family. She loved her job, but looking ahead, she could see no end to the time pressures caused by its demands. At that moment, she decided that she had to—and wanted to—make a change to allocate more time to her family.

You may have recognized something about yourself and the way you're living in one of these examples, and your own story may reveal other factors that motivate you to repot. You might feel that you'd like to make a change, but your garden is so well established and tending it is taking so much of your time and energy that you're reluctant to undertake anything new. Look more closely, however. . . . Is it time for you to redesign the landscape of your own life?

Exercise: The Repotting-Readiness Index

To help you determine if you're ready to repot, we've developed this three-step exercise. (Use your *Repotting 101 Workbook* for all the exercises in this book, or follow the instructions to complete the ones in this chapter.) As hard as it may be to take an honest look at your life, it's important for you to set aside some time to answer these questions. Chris, the publisher who wanted to repot, took three years to evaluate her need for change because she didn't have a plan. Our exercises will give you a reality check on how you spend your time, something you'll need to be aware of if you want to redesign your landscape.

The first step of the exercise involves filling out a simple checklist that will help you tap into your feelings about how you spend your time. If three or more of your answers are *Yes* (whether you answered *Yes, daily; Yes, weekly;* or even just *Yes, monthly*), you're probably ready to repot.

The second step—creating and surveying your current Personal Garden Calendar—will help you understand how you're spending your time by making you focus on "have to" versus "want to" commitments. If the majority of your day, week, or month is consumed with "must do/have to" and "don't want to" activities, you may need to consider how you might better incorporate your values and priorities into your schedule.

The third step—the trade-off test—will help you weigh whether repotting is worth the cost of lost opportunities. Remember, every choice you make entails loss as well as gain. Understanding the upsides and downsides of your options is important if you want to create a repotting mind-set.

Step 1: The Checklist

In our *Repotting 101 Workbook* or your notebook, answer each question below with: *No; Yes, monthly; Yes, weekly;* or *Yes, daily.*

1. When you have moments of downtime for reflection, do you have a lingering sense of unease about the direction of your life?

2. Do you spend a disproportionate amount of time on activities that aren't rewarding or that deplete your energy level?

3. Do you feel you're shortchanging key relationships (with friends, husband, children, parents, other family members, colleagues, pets, and so on)?

4. Do you sometimes wish that a greater percentage of your busy schedule could be devoted to activities that would make your life feel more meaningful (such as supporting a cause, helping an elderly parent or a friend in need, spending time in your garden, and the like)?

5. Do you feel that time is passing and you're missing opportunities to grow because your day-to-day focus is too narrow?

6. Do you feel as if your internal clock is frozen in time because you've given up on growing and learning new things?

7. Does it seem as though you have no time for yourself: for maintaining your personal health, managing projects (such as organizing your home office, closets, or photo collections), travel, or educational pursuits?

8. If you have a career, is it still meeting your needs? For example, do you enjoy the work, do you feel valued, is there opportunity for advancement, does it fit with your overall lifestyle, and so on?

(For questions 9 and 10, just answer *Yes* or *No*.)

9. If you don't have a career, is your life still meeting your needs? For example, are you interested in working on a meaningful project (volunteering, writing, painting, and the like)? Do you have time to work from home or outside the home, start a business or franchise, embark on a spiritual or cultural journey, or some other similar venture?

10. Do you feel that you never get enough sleep? Do you wake up tired or lack energy during the day? Is sleep the first thing to be sacrificed and last thing to be checked off your list?

11. Is your overall sense that whatever the components of your life are, the current mix isn't fulfilling for you?

12. Do you feel overwhelmed? Does it seem as though there's too much pressure on you and you're ready for a meltdown?

How did you do? How many *Yes* answers did you have? Because these questions raise such key issues, even one affirmative response may be cause for you to reflect on your personal landscape. Although there's no magic number that indicates you definitely must repot, if you answered *Yes* to three or more questions—even if it was only *Yes, monthly*—your personal garden may need attention now. Your daily life may not be in sync with your values. If so, there's a disconnect between your interior self and your external life. It's time to put your schedule under the microscope.

Step 2: Time Tracking

This exercise will help you survey your current Personal Garden Calendar, providing a reality check that will allow you to see how you're spending every hour in a month. Follow the steps below in this exercise—no fudging! You'll need four colored pens (black, blue, green, and red) and the calendar in the *Repotting 101 Workbook* or a blank monthly calendar showing an hourly breakdown of each day in a four-week period.

1. Fill in the blocks of time according to how you spend them. You may be doing any of the following: working, caring for and transporting children, tending to elderly parents, exercising, volunteering, seeing the doctor or dentist, reading, sleeping, running errands, taking part in social events, engaging in spiritual pursuits, participating in educational activities, cooking or providing meals, eating, attending to personal hygiene, taking care of pets, playing sports, surfing the Internet, chatting online, shopping (for necessities or pleasure), enjoying entertainment, attending meetings (community, school, church, or other), doing household chores, indulging in hobbies, traveling, engaging in cultural activities, and so on. Be accurate and specific.

2. Evaluate your current Personal Garden Calendar according to the criteria that follow. (Note that some blocks of time may fit into more than one category.)

- **Must do/have to.** These are essential activities that can't be avoided, such as eating, sleeping, working, or providing child care. Circle everything in this group with a *black* pen or marker.

- **Need to.** This category includes activities you've determined are good for you and need to be done (such as exercising and engaging in spiritual pursuits) or that you're passionate about (such as playing music, painting, or doing volunteer work). Circle all of these with a *blue* pen or marker.

- **Want to.** These are the events you enjoy and choose to engage in (such as getting a massage, watching movies, spending time with family and friends, and so on). Circle these with a *green* pen or marker.

- **Don't want to.** These engagements are the ones that you wish you could avoid entirely (such as working at an unfulfilling job, attending the office cocktail party or another social commitment you don't enjoy, spending time with people you don't like but feel obligated to socialize with, doing household chores, and so on). Circle these activities with a *red* pen or marker.

Which colors are most prominent in your schedule? If a majority of your time is outlined in black or red, it may be time for a major life adjustment. Let's look more closely at your Personal Garden Calendar, because if your goal is to find more time, every one of your activities must be scrutinized. Add up the number of hours you spend on each category.

— For the **must do/have to** activities, ask yourself these questions: *Am I sure that everything marked in black is essential? Is it feasible to outsource any of these required tasks or find alternative solutions?* For example, if you're spending two hours a day on business lunches, could you brown-bag it occasionally?

— For the **need to** list, ask yourself: *Are these activities still fulfilling my original goals?* For instance, is your book group still providing mental and social stimulation? Is there a better way to support your child's school than attending committee meetings and bake sales?

— Is your **want to** list up to date? Do you have enough time to pursue things you enjoy? If this section has become overgrown, is it time to weed out the activities you don't enjoy as much in order to allow time for truly enjoyable pursuits to flourish?

— The **don't want to** category presents the most challenges. You may be spending time on activities or relationships that you feel are dreaded obligations. Do you need to make some hard choices? If you're in a job that makes you unhappy, extricating yourself from it will require a major commitment of time and resources. The same holds true for personal relationships that are no longer working for you. In the case of household chores, is it possible to get yourself out from under some of them by delegating them to family members, hiring someone to do them, or simply letting go? You might want to lower your standards, tolerating a less-than-perfect home or cooking fewer meals from scratch.

Step 3: The Trade-off Test

This will help you weigh the costs of the opportunities that you have before you. The "no boundaries" mind-set of 21st-century women has both positive and negative aspects. On the one hand, women like you see a horizon of endless possibilities; you may have the luxury of choosing from myriad options in all facets of your life. On the other hand, having so many choices can create overload, and the inability to sort out which options are the best for you can create stress.

The finest gardens aren't the ones chock-full of shrubs and seedlings, but those that provide enough open space to allow each plant to flourish and be a focal point. Rather than assuming that you should do as much as possible, you need to ask yourself whether less is more. After completing the work thus far, you can probably see areas in your life that need attention. But with every change, there's a trade-off. The exercise below is intended to help you evaluate your own compromises in making whatever change you choose. Use your *Repotting 101 Workbook* or your own materials.

Determining and Evaluating Trade-offs

Use the appropriate page in *Repotting 101* or divide a piece of paper into two columns. In the first column, list potential gains from making a particular change; and in the second, write down possible losses or downsides. Think about the trade-offs you'd make if you were planting a garden. If you put annuals throughout your plot, you'd enjoy their fabulous colors in the spring, summer, and fall. But if you were to plant *only* annuals and no evergreens, what would happen to the overall look of your garden in the winter?

In the same way, if you're currently working and you want to start a family, you may need to weigh the potential loss of income and status against having more time at home and achieving the self-fulfillment that can come from mothering. If you're currently at home and are contemplating a new identity as a community leader, you'll have to consider the reality of having less time to devote to your family versus the benefit of a new and stimulating pursuit.

When looking at the pros and cons of making a particular change, keep in mind that there are more factors to consider than how much time or money it will cost you. If you go back to school full-time, you may be giving up vacations with your family in order to study, but the upside could be a greater sense of fulfillment or the ability to advance your career. If you choose some other endeavor, there may be additional lost opportunities that you have to be willing and ready to give up.

When you see what the possible consequences are, ask yourself: *Am I ready and willing to accept the losses or downsides that will result from making this change? Are the upsides great enough to warrant the disruption or sacrifices involved?*

What's your conclusion at this stage of your journey? Are you ready to change or not? By closely examining your daily activities, you've taken an important first step in determining if you need, want, and are ready to create a new identity for yourself.

What may become startlingly clear is that you're not a candidate for repotting at this time. The trade-offs may be too high, or your motivation may not be strong enough to take you through this transformative process. Alternatively, you may see on paper for the first time that it's the right season for you to transplant yourself or at least undertake a partial repotting.

Personal Gardening Tip: Take time to make time. Before you can repot, you need to understand how you currently spend your days, weeks, and months. Decide what needs to be changed in your Personal Garden Calendar and what trade-offs you'll have to make.

No matter what the results of the three previous exercises revealed to you, read on. In the following chapters, we're going to continue to examine the elements of repotting. Since how you spend your time is a reflection of what's good and bad, right and wrong, and valuable and extraneous in your life, let's take a closer look at the time issue, and how it impacts your perceptions of your world.

Chapter Two

Do You Need More Space Around You?

Time is the central focus of a woman's life: spending it, managing it, and finding more of it. The U.S. Department of Labor's Bureau of Labor Statistics has even developed a new American Time Use Survey to calculate how Americans spend a critical resource: their time. In a different survey in 2004, three-quarters of women who were 40 to 54 years old said that life is much too complicated. More than 50 percent of respondents in yet another survey reported that they work in bed at least once a week.

The old nine-to-five, Monday-through-Friday work-week is no longer the norm; only about 30 percent of U.S. workers have this "standard" workday schedule. As of 2002, nearly 40 percent of employed Americans said that they worked during the evening, weekends, overnight, or on a rotating shift. And in a *Wall Street Journal* article, a University of Maryland sociology professor declared, "Nonstandard and weekend work is here to stay." Given these facts, it's no surprise that a majority of women cite fatigue or lack of energy as their number one complaint.

The marketplace has responded to this "meltdown mentality" trend by offering time-saving solutions. From express workouts of 30 minutes or less; to the phenomenal growth of online shopping; to the enormous increase in the sale of PDAs, walkie-talkies, and multitasking cell phones, consumers now have access to many shortcuts to save time. Stay-at-home mothers often use the Internet to replace physical interaction with other moms, a trend called "the mommy-tech wave," according to a *New York Times* article.

Even these technology time-savers are becoming obsolete as a new generation of office workers who grew up with instant messaging has entered the workplace. The *New York Times* noted that these younger workers have made instant messaging the "new black"—the latest trend in information technology.

These innovations are meant to help consumers save time and frequently achieve that goal. Using all these gadgets, however, can actually eat up the day. Managing e-mail, text messages, and other forms of incoming information can be distracting, time-consuming, and place yet another demand on users. So despite the many gadgets available, women *still* feel they don't have enough hours to get everything done.

The time equation—how time is allocated, spent, and valued—is a major concern for women in the new millennium. Our transformed view of time comes in part from revolutionary changes associated with the high-tech world. To cope with the challenges of the age we live in, the warp-speed pace of incoming information, and multiple demands, many women are trying to develop a survival strategy by creating a time cocoon—a buffer between their environment and the world at large.

These struggles have women stressed out and searching for pockets of respite; they're a driving force behind the decision to change gears and repot. Instead of fulfilling a schedule, many women are now determined to fulfill their goals. The old concept of leisure has been transformed into the idea of discretionary moments: Women find pockets of time to spend on things they feel are important, such as family activities, reading, or self-improvement. More and more, luxury today is defined as time prosperity, having open periods of time that aren't committed to anything or anyone else.

This chapter will show you how to take a proactive approach toward creating the time needed for changing your life. You'll learn how to create the necessary "space" around yourself to accomplish two essential personal landscape activities: reflecting on what matters to you and creating a personal Time Savings Bank by taking a hard-nosed approach to editing your daily to-do list. These activities will allow you to initiate the repotting process.

Changing Your Time Mind-set

Think about your garden-planning process. You'll recall that the first step in creating your design program is establishing your baseline requirements, which means taking an inventory of all the components of your life and how much time they require. The only way to create enough space for your new lifestyle is to edit unnecessary time eaters out of your calendar.

Whether it's your backyard or flower boxes on your deck, you've probably learned by now that jamming too many plants in one place may kill them or stifle new growth. We know that living things need enough space around them to flourish. The lives of many of the women we interviewed were so overscheduled that they had no time or energy for reflection, planning, or beginning to explore new directions.

We recognize that revamping your schedule in the face of the daily onslaught of responsibilities and opportunities is an uphill battle. If you undertake any significant change in your life—for instance, beginning a new job, starting a family, moving, or attending school—you'll need to make emotional and mental commitments to reach your goals. To begin the process of redesigning your life, you must change your mind-set. When you survey your current calendar, remember that after you've allotted time for what's essential, everything else is up for grabs and can be dropped from your to-do list.

Biba's Story: Changing Her Time Outlook

Biba is a good example of a woman who had to completely change her attitude about time in order to live the way she wanted to. A former professional volleyball player from Russia, she entered the business world in New York as a currency trader. She then moved to California to take a financial analyst's job and married a colleague with a young child from a previous marriage.

Even though her new family and attendant responsibilities significantly affected her schedule, Biba continued to try to live her life as a financial analyst 24/7. Tracking global markets at 3 A.M. didn't leave her much opportunity or energy to manage her new home life, so she stopped working and gradually began to focus on finding a new outlook toward time and her relationship to it. She recognized that her trading mentality, focusing on nano-second buying and selling at all hours of the day and night, wasn't conducive to being a wife, raising a child, or participating in her community. She needed to slow down and create a new time mind-set.

Exercise: Focus on Your Time Mind-Set

Let's look at your life as if it were a journal—every week, you're writing a chapter. Are your priorities a foot-note, or are they part of the main text? In order to make whatever changes you want, you'll need to discipline yourself to review your schedule every week or month. This is nonnegotiable. Just as you're committed to eating properly, walking your dog, or reading a bedtime story to your children, you need to dedicate yourself to making the time to reflect on how you use each day.

1. Keep track of your time in your Personal Garden Calendar. Pull out your repotting equipment—the *Repotting 101 Workbook* or whatever you've previously used to do your exercises. Each day, jot down any reactions you have to specific activities or events as they occur. Before going to bed, look back at each reaction you listed and ask yourself, *Why did I respond that way?* Do you come away from some activities with a sense of relief that they're over or feeling as though they were a waste of time? Note, too, those pursuits that made you feel enriched, happy, fulfilled, or energized. Write it all down. (You may find it helpful to do this activity every day for a week).

2. Reflect on how you spend your time. At the end of the month, look back on what you've written in your *Repotting 101 Workbook* or journal. Are you beginning to see a pattern? For instance, do all of your outdoor activities energize you? Are some of your social obligations making you feel resentful? Do you wish that you could make your commute more productive?

This exercise lays the groundwork for the two following ones: weeding your garden beds to create a Time Savings Bank and creating more space in your personal garden by adding new, unplanted plots. Keep your workbook or journal in a handy place; you'll want to refer to it as you read the chapters that follow.

Now that you're working on developing a new time mind-set, you can move on to the next exercise.

Exercise: Weeding Your Garden Beds to Create a Time Savings Bank

The purpose of this exercise is to help you define what you find essential so that you can weed out what you don't need. You'll be looking more carefully at how you defined your activities back in Chapter 1. When you complete this evaluation, you may have to make adjustments to your schedule, creating a Time Savings Bank (which is what you'll do in the exercise that follows this one). For instance, you might want to eliminate some of your Have To activities. *Remember, if you want to reshape your garden, you must get a new perspective.* Just as plants with cramped roots won't grow or blossom, neither can you flourish in an overscheduled life.

Step 1

Scan the Personal Garden Calendar that you created in your *Repotting 101 Workbook* or notebook in Chapter 1, going through all the items on it in this order:

— **Focus on the Must Do/Have To activities.** Confirm to yourself that everything listed in these categories is indispensable and worth the time you're spending. Can you be scheduling your life or your family's time more efficiently? For example, is it possible to schedule back-to-back appointments rather than making two trips?

— **Focus on the Don't Want To activities.** How many of these can be eliminated without major disruption or a negative impact on you or others? Start small by looking at nonessentials. Are you doing these things out of habit? Eliminating less important commitments first will provide you with space for reflection and considering what activities you'd prefer to engage in. For instance, are you spending more time dealing with a relative's problems than your own?

— **Focus on the Need To list.** Do you have too many items on this list? Have you really thought about your priorities? If, for instance, you feel that you need fitness activities to fulfill your health and social needs, can you accomplish this goal with just one sport or type of class instead of three?

— **Focus on your Want To list.** Is it realistic? Is it so long that you never get to complete most of the items on it? Even though your interests may have changed, do you keep doing the same things? For instance, is the time you spend at your monthly lunch with friends still meeting your social needs? Are multiple trips for beauty treatments taking too much time and not relaxing you? Eliminate anything that doesn't meet your needs.

Step 2

Create one list of essential activities and another of optional activities:

— Go through every activity in each of the categories from Step 1 and cull those that remain essential. Write the "keepers" on the appropriate page in your *Repotting 101 Workbook,* or make two columns on a blank sheet of paper. List your essential activities in one column and the optional ones in the other. You may see that some things no longer fit in with your new time mindset. If so, eliminate them now. This will help you create your personal Time Savings Bank.

— Do a cost-benefit analysis. Ask yourself if the time commitment each activity takes is at least equal to the benefit you receive from it. Grade each activity using this scale:

A = Valuable/essential (can't do without it)

B = Not vital but offers emotional, financial, or other important rewards

C = Provides little or no benefit

Step 3

Apply the gardening technique of deadheading (clipping faded flowers from plants) to your schedule:

— Just as you'd remove spent blooms to promote further growth and blossoms in your garden, you need to **cut off activities if their costs outweigh their benefits.** You need to *eliminate* everything that you assigned a grade of C.

— **Create a new list of your activities without the C's.** Calculate the amount of time you've saved by weeding out the low scorers. You've now created new space in your Personal Garden Calendar.

An Essential Tool:
Your _Revised_ Personal Garden Calendar

You've weeded your life's garden to create more space and time for yourself. The result of your efforts in this exercise is a *revised* Personal Garden Calendar. This is an essential repotting tool that you'll need to refer to (and possibly revise again) as you follow the repotting program outlined in the remaining chapters. Remember, you can't move on to the next step unless you've created a totally accurate picture of how you want to spend your time.

Deb's Story: Pushing the
Pause Button on a Spin-Cycle Life

Sometimes you have to stop before you can go. Deb is a perfect example of someone who had to prune her life, create a personal time oasis for reflection, and then act on her new goals.

Deb spent ten years on the fast track in the fashion world in New York City. After her marriage brought her to Washington, D.C., she maintained her career by commuting to New York and spending one week a month there. On top of this draining commute, she was also managing three households—a New York apartment, a Washington house, and another residence in southern Virginia where her husband's business was headquartered. When she became pregnant with her first child, she continued this spin-cycle life, but the birth of two more children in a three-year period meant something had to give.

At this point, Deb had to carve out time to reflect on how she was going to raise a family and continue some sort of professional life without her world becoming unglued. From an early age, she knew that her touchstone in life was her love of color, design, and fashion. No matter where she lived, she needed to keep this as part of her life's landscape.

This repotter had come to the point in her life where she needed to create a personal time oasis. By eliminating the New York commute and everything it entailed, Deb was able to find time to listen to her inner self. After two years in Washington as a "conscientious objector"—her term for not wanting to be in that city—she had to find a way to make a life there. In other words, she had to create a new design for her personal garden.

She surveyed all the important components of her life (family, passions, and career) to determine what needed to be weeded out and what needed to stay and grow. Once Deb made the decision to center her life in one location—Washington, D.C.—she was able to move forward.

This repotting process did not occur overnight and required sacrifice and courage on Deb's part. Removing the time-eating responsibilities in New York City from her life provided her with a personal time oasis in which she could plan and carry out the next steps in the process of redesigning her garden. While she wanted to keep her old identity as a fashion consultant in New York, Deb knew that putting her family first would necessitate creating a new version of her career in Washington. By eliminating her commute and thereby adding hours to her Time Savings Bank, Deb was able to begin a successful transition to a better family life and career in her new home.

Exercise: Adding New Garden Beds—
Creating More Space in Your Garden

Getting rid of the obvious weeds in your personal garden is relatively easy. You may want to use the oasis you created to reflect on redesigning your life, think about other ways to make your time go further, and lessen your overall stress. Here are ideas for additional ways to create more space in your garden:

— **Outsource activities.** You can delegate to family members or paid helpers or use community resources to get the job done. Invest time in training your children (especially teens) to do more household chores, from watering plants to emptying wastebaskets to doing laundry. Pay a neighborhood teen to care for your pet or hire a dog walker to do so. Investigate services for seniors that can relieve you of some of your responsibilities to your aging parents, from food delivery to art classes.

— **"Thin-slice" some activities—that is, use shortcuts when possible to be more efficient.** Let go of the perfectionist mentality. You don't have to manage every detail in your life or that of your family. Consolidate bill paying, note writing, form processing, and similar tasks and do them all once a week or once a month, depending on your needs. Use your fitness club's on-site dry cleaners rather than dropping your clothes at a separate establishment (thus having to make an extra trip); try an Internet grocery order and delivery service. Barter services with your friends, family members, and neighbors—for instance, can you exchange weekday child-care or pet-sitting for reciprocal services during your weekends away?

— **Put some activities on autopilot.** Postpone projects that aren't time sensitive or critical in favor of creating more opportunities for personal reflection. Do you really need to start painting the front hall this month? Schedule these nonessential projects for specific dates in the future to free up more time now for contemplation.

— **Prune your social calendar.** Edit out social activities that aren't positive additions to your day, week, month . . . or *life!* Just because you've been doing something for a regular basis for a long time doesn't mean it has to remain part of your schedule forever.

— **Let fallow beds lie.** Don't immediately fill in the open spaces on your revised Personal Garden Calendar—just say *"No!"* You may feel pressure from within yourself and from others to substitute new activities for those you've eliminated. Don't let family members or friends make you feel guilty if you don't take on projects and responsibilities just to fill your new blocks of free time. Giving yourself openings in your schedule for reflection creates room to "breathe"—so recognize that creating open space on your calendar is valuable and essential.

Sherry's Story: Single and Overwhelmed

Sherry, a young, single nurse practitioner living in a metropolitan area, was trying to make more time to contemplate changes in her career. The demands of her emotionally draining job and caring for her apartment, cat, and ailing mother (who was 20 miles away) meant that at the end of each week, she had no energy or time to focus on immediate or long-term plans in her life.

With no chance to pursue a social life, not to mention research a much-needed vacation, Sherry had to find ways to create a personal time oasis. She began by identifying a local community-based program to provide some meals to her mother. When she looked at the trade-off—her commute; the price of gasoline; and most important, the personal costs in feeling stressed and under constant obligation to her mother—she realized that the six or more hours she saved for herself by outsourcing her mother's meals three days a week was well worth it. Sherry was almost delirious with the prospect of having more free time, although she continued to call and visit her mother once a week.

But she wasn't immediately able to use those hours toward her main goal of analyzing her career path. Indeed, when a friend asked her to join a theater production, which required six hours a week of volunteering, she was tempted to jump right in. But instead of allowing herself to be diverted for whatever reasons, our advice to Sherry was to let her newly fallow bed lie. We felt she shouldn't rush to fill the vacuum she'd created.

Sherry had taken two important steps:

1.   She recognized her time problem: Her over-scheduled life didn't allow time for any reflection.

2.   She made space in her schedule through out-sourcing some of her mother's meals.

But she still needed to take the third and most essential step:

3.   Retain enough of her free time so that she could get started on her master landscape plan.

This was our proposed solution: Out of her six reclaimed hours, Sherry should use one hour a week to research travel plans or gather other information on topics of interest, information that would help her determine how to spend the time she'd freed up. Another hour could be spent on a leisure activity for relaxation, such as swimming or yoga. But we advised her to spend the majority of her new free time—four hours per week—dealing with the critical task of developing her "base plan" for changing her career, a pursuit that was very important to her.

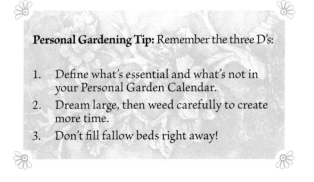

Personal Gardening Tip: Remember the three D's:

1. Define what's essential and what's not in your Personal Garden Calendar.
2. Dream large, then weed carefully to create more time.
3. Don't fill fallow beds right away!

Creating "space" around you is only the first step in deciding whether you're ready to repot. The next chapter will help you find the sunlight in your garden. For repotters, the term *sunlight* means your overall sense of health and well-being. You'll learn the steps you need to take to nourish your garden and create a healthy environment that will enable you to grow!

Chapter Three

Do You Need More Light?

A landscape designer knows that sunlight is essential for the health of all garden greenery. Without it, there can be no photosynthesis, growth, or blossoms; plants will wilt and die. In planning or changing a garden, one of the first things a gardener must do is to evaluate the amount of light that's available and how different species will respond to it. Getting the right mix of sun and shade will allow different types of plants to flourish.

In your personal garden, getting the right amount of light means managing the state of your overall health. This isn't merely the absence of disease or infirmity; it's a state of physical, mental, social, and spiritual well-being. In more than 15 years of research across the country, we found that health is a central focus in the lives of women, and that it's fundamental to the ability to start the repotting process.

In this chapter, we'll discuss how finding the right amount of "light"—health and well-being—is key to the growth of your personal garden. Your current lifestyle can either help or hinder your efforts. In the following sections, we'll help you learn how to:

- **Survey** your physical, mental, and spiritual landscape to see what needs attention

- **Identify** your stress hot buttons so that you can remove barriers to wellness

- **Visualize** your ideal garden to bring more light into your life

Focus on Your Inner Garden: Your Body

Gardeners research every aspect of a landscape before they begin the design or redesign process. This attention to natural factors—soil, sun, shade, water, wind patterns, and existing plantings—allows them to assess the physical health of the environment. To successfully repot, you need to check the status of your physical well-being by surveying your daily nutrition, exercise, and sleep patterns. In addition, periodic health issues—such as eye problems or an aching hip—should be addressed as they arise.

Let's start with a nutrition checkup. Perhaps you need to zero in on the role food plays in your life, looking at everything from "dashboard dining" to skipping meals to overeating. In spite of the 360-degree media onslaught of information about food, supplements, and diets, women are still confused about what's the best recipe for their own nutritional needs.

For example, recent studies discount the relationship between longevity and low-fat diets, the exact opposite of earlier research. Taking calcium supplements is no longer seen as a protective measure against bone loss and osteoporosis, according to a *Wall Street Journal* article. And it was noted in another article that even the benefits of soy are in question. As one woman told us, "I feel like I'm experiencing whiplash—one day I read that soy is good for you, and the next day it's bad. I don't know where to turn, or what to think."

Keep in mind that you're a combination of what you eat and your genetic history. You can't change your DNA, but you can control your daily nutritional intake. Just as plants in your garden require the proper mix of nutrients in the soil in order to grow, you need a good foundation to provide the sense of well-being and energy you need to repot. Whether you use the Internet to research and track your nutrition and diet or work with a counselor to create a plan, you need to focus on this aspect of your health. It may mean adjusting your schedule, making time to cook healthier meals instead of eating takeout, or using prepared meals from companies such as the Zone Diet, eDiets.com, and the like.

Today, most women understand the link between physical activity and their overall health. Indeed, according to a recent study by the American Cancer Society, as many as half of all cancer deaths could be prevented if more people made lifestyle changes such as eating nutritiously and getting regular exercise and recommended health screenings. How are you maintaining your body—through an exercise regimen, a yoga or Pilates class, walking your dog, or swimming laps? Or maybe all you have time for is climbing stairs or walking in the mall on your lunch break.

Some individuals lack the motivation to keep moving on their own. A University of Nebraska study has shown that it's easier for women to keep up a routine if they have a partner to exercise with. In addition, women's time crunch often interferes with their intended schedule; even the most dedicated exercisers sometimes miss their daily ritual, whether due to business travel or other obligations.

For some women, the only break in an otherwise frantic routine may be a 20-minute walk with headphones on. As a single mother in Los Angeles told us, "My only private time in the day—my escape from family and work—is when I walk at the track near my house. I try never to miss this." But it's a given that women can't function—or repot—at their optimal level if they aren't physically active.

In addition to needing daily exercise, you must look carefully at your sleep regimen. With almost half of all Americans reporting that they don't get enough rest, women are especially deprived due to their multitasking tendencies. According to Dr. James B. Maas, Cornell University Professor of Psychology, sleep expert, and the author of *Power Sleep,* "The quantity and quality of your sleep, in large measure, will determine the success of your waking life. It will affect your mood, energy, alertness, productivity, sense of well-being, and longevity. Sleep is a necessity, not a luxury. For women, healthy sleep is essential."

Health maintenance also requires preventive care. Many women tend to put themselves last in their list of priorities, after family and even their pets. Financial or cultural reasons may be the cause, but in many cases women postpone regular checkups due to lack of time or focus.

One executive who worked with global financial markets and was married with three children never made time for health maintenance. She paid the price for her workaholic lifestyle when she was diagnosed with late-stage non-Hodgkin's lymphoma. She told us, "My illness was the worst kind of wake-up call; I paid the price for putting my health and well-being last."

Some experts disagree about the benefits of yearly exams, but are you listening to your body? If something is wrong, are you getting it checked out? If you're over 50 years old, have you had basic tests to serve as a baseline for future care and maintenance? These are examples of health issues you may want to review as you determine your physical readiness to repot.

Repot Your Body: Do a "Body Scan"

Clinics that provide body-scanning techniques to give consumers a full picture of every detail of their physical state at a particular point in time have sprung up across America. These businesses are indicative of the new self-care mind-set. But when *we* advocate doing a body scan, we're not recommending that you spend your time or money on a clinical procedure; we're asking you to take the time to listen to your physical self. Look at yourself from head to toe, and consider whether your current exercise, nutrition, sleep, and health regimens are what they should be. Are you safeguarding your overall well-being? You may need to adopt a new mind-set to put these health components front and center in your life. *Remember, you control the amount of time you spend on yourself.*

Hilda's Story

Hilda, a Hispanic mother of three who's in her 40s, is a perfect example of a woman who needs to make more time for physical activity. In addition to being a mom, she runs a day-care center from her home, has been taking computer classes before starting her business each morning, and does weekend work for another family. She needs energy but has none left after her nonstop schedule. She also wants to lose weight.

Hilda is grappling with how to carve out even a small amount of time for some kind of exercise. Acknowledging that she needs some time in her day for "light" was an important first step, but now she must maintain a mental commitment to her health and find opportunities to take care of herself. Our proposed solution was that she allocate an extra 15 or 30 minutes each day to physical activities.

Hilda has decided that once her computer courses are finished, she'll hold on to the time she has created to improve her skills and use it to walk in her neighborhood. It's a good strategy: A recent study by the University of Missouri-Columbia revealed that previously inactive people who walked five times a week for 20 minutes lost an average of 14 pounds in a year.

Exercise: The Body Scan

You can initiate your own preliminary "body scan" by completing this section. To do this and the other exercises in this chapter, you'll need to refer to the new time blocks you created on your revised Personal Garden Calendar in Chapter 2.

Ask yourself the following questions and write your answers in your *Repotting 101 Workbook* or wherever you've been keeping your notes.

1. Calculate how much time you've allocated for exercise. When you revised your Personal Garden Calendar, did you alter the amount of time you were going to dedicate to fitness (adding or subtracting time or maintaining the status quo)?

2. Is your current exercise regimen meeting your needs in terms of your energy level, your sense of well-being, your age, and your overall weight and fitness goals? Have you considered new ways to fit movement into your day; accommodate a changing schedule; or address factors such as menopause, injury, or illness? If, for instance, you love swimming but find that changing clothes, drying your hair, and so on is too time-consuming, then you may want to substitute jogging near your home or attending an on-site exercise class at work.

3. Do you feel that your current eating patterns are meeting your energy and nutritional needs? If you rely on "grab 'n' go" food solutions for two out of three meals per day, perhaps you should consider keeping a food journal. Jot down your daily intake for one week. Is breakfast a bagel and coffee or a drinkable yogurt? Are you eating a candy bar for lunch? Be honest!

4. Are you making the best choices to provide your body with the fuel and nutrition it needs each day? Are you eating high-sodium beef jerky for a quick boost instead of a healthier energy bar or handful of unsalted

nuts? You can use the Web as a resource to help you balance your daily caloric intake and make better choices, or you can consult one of many books on this subject.

5. Are you comfortable with the amount of sleep you're getting each night? If you're one of the many Americans who have issues in this area (such as not getting enough rest or suffering from insomnia), then you probably can't function at an optimal level during the day. For instance, do you feel that your level of alertness is diminished due to lack of sleep? Is your judgment impaired? Are you often moody? Review your revised Personal Garden Calendar and determine how much sleep you're getting. Do you want or need to further alter your schedule in order to get more?

6. Have you reviewed all the factors that might be contributing to your lack of sleep? Look at this checklist and decide which items you can control:

- **Caffeine:** Are you getting too much or consuming it too late in the day?

- **TV:** Are you watching from your bed instead of sleeping?

- **Sleep environment:** Do you have the right pillow and mattress and comfortable levels of darkness, noise, and room temperature?

- **Working/reading in bed:** Do you work or read in bed too much, too late, or too often?

- **Computer habits:** Are you using this tool too much? Are you spending a lot of time online at home for work, e-mail, or games? Have you set limits for yourself in this area?

- **Bedtime rituals:** Are they geared toward turning down the volume of your day? Are you revving up instead of winding down?

7. If you can't find additional hours each night to sleep, for whatever reason, what stopgap measures could you use to increase your daily rest? For instance, what about taking a 20-minute power nap instead of going to lunch with colleagues? Have you considered capitalizing on your children's naps to create your own downtime? How about taking a ten-minute respite to read or meditate rather than frantically filling the time with another task?

8. Are you up to date on all the minimum basic health-maintenance checkups, tests, and consultations appropriate for your age and life stage? For instance, are the nooks and crannies of your handbag and desk filled with referral slips for various tests that you haven't gotten around to scheduling? Has your eczema or anti-allergy prescription expired but you haven't seen the doctor yet? How long has it been since you last got your teeth cleaned?

9. Are you spending more time on beauty treatments that address your outer appearance than you are on the state of your inner health? Take a close look at your revised Personal Garden Calendar. Do you need to change

the ratio of time spent on "surface" regimens (such as facials and manicures) versus time spent on medical checkups or healthy rituals (such as daily exercise)?

Repot Your Mind

Now that you've reviewed your physical state to determine whether you need to make changes in your diet, exercise, and sleep regimens to create more "light" for yourself, it's time to survey your mental and emotional landscape. For women, this requires light as well. You need peace of mind and a sense of being in control even when everything isn't in perfect order. The growth in the number of day spas—which has almost doubled in the past four years—is a clear indication of women's increasing desire to find respite in their daily lives. Sales of prescription anti-anxiety and sleep-inducing drugs are also exploding because people are seeking solutions for their stress.

Understanding the causes of this tension and helping women deal with it has become a major focus of researchers and scientists. A new saliva test can gauge a woman's stress level by measuring her hormonal levels, and other methods are being developed to reveal whether there's a genetic propensity for stress. The psychology of stress is also being closely studied. Suzanne Ouellette, Ph.D., a professor at the Graduate Center at the City University of New York, has developed a stress hardiness scale to determine how resilient people are. She noted, "Stress hardiness reflects a fundamental stance in life that expresses commitment, control, and readiness to respond to challenge." People who score high find change interesting and an incentive toward growth rather than a threat to their security.

Schedules today are overloaded, uneven, and filled with the unexpected, and developing stress hardiness greatly contributes to mental well-being. The inability to deal with the roller coaster of life can leave some women totally immobilized, barely able to get through their routines, much less able to design a new future for themselves. It can also negatively impact health. Research from Northwestern University in Chicago indicates that women who race through the day are twice as likely to develop high blood pressure.

Boomer women are experiencing increasing stress due to their position as the "sandwich generation," taking care of their own children as well as aging relatives. Research done by Brenda Spillman and Kirsten Black of the Urban Institute shows that in 1999, two-thirds of older people with disabilities relied solely on family for care, and 56 percent of nonprofessional caregivers had experienced anxiety or depression in the previous six months. For these women, finding respite from the stress of their responsibilities is essential for mental health.

Your tension may also be caused by constant multitasking, since this can actually inhibit your ability to focus and think clearly. Recent research has revealed a decline in participants' cognitive function due to multitasking. People who were able to focus on one thing at a time performed better than those whose brains were overextended. Reducing stress to improve your mental and emotional well-being provides light that will help your growth process as you repot.

Most plants can't grow in continual direct sunlight or in total darkness; they need a mix of light and shade.

As you look at your mental and emotional well-being, you, too, need to have a mix—in other words, a balanced perspective. You can't necessarily balance your life on a daily basis, but it's important to maintain a mental and emotional equilibrium overall because it will allow you to function at your optimal level. We know that you may be facing issues that aren't going to disappear overnight, but how you respond to them will affect your well-being, and that's what we want you to focus on.

Exercise: The Mind Scan

To diagnose your current mind-set, do this exercise, which will help you evaluate your mental and emotional readiness to repot. You can answer these questions in your *Repotting 101 Workbook* or use your own materials.

1. Do you suffer from the "ricochet effect"? In other words, does your mind constantly bounce from one thought to the next, leaving you feeling unfocused? Have you overscheduled your children with too many play-dates or activities so that each day is a marathon race to dinnertime? Have you allowed your work life to spill over into your home life so that there's no respite?

2. Are you letting your personal garden become overgrown because you're mentally and emotionally drifting? Are you allowing your schedule and daily activities to drive you instead of taking control of your life? Is your brain so overloaded that you're suffering from a lack of mental direction at home or work?

3. Has your mind atrophied from use or overuse of technology? We're all aware of the benefits of increased and faster communication through cell phones, PDAs, computers, instant messaging (IM), and the like. However, there's a price you pay when you overuse those helpers. Accessing and sifting through the onslaught of information is time-consuming and may even cloud your mental capabilities and thought processes. You need to compare the perceived benefits of using technology with the costs to your mental state. Checking e-mail, browsing the Web, playing solitaire and other games, and talking on your cell phone can be mental distractions.

4. Have you become so dependent upon your electronic address book or calendar that you don't know your schedule or any phone numbers without consulting your PDA? Is it time for you to get out of your electronic haze to engage in some real-life thinking and planning? Can you make a critical appraisal of your schedule if it's only on your PDA and not in your brain?

5. Do you feel that you lack control over your life? Do you experience this sensation daily, weekly, or monthly? Do seasons or even years go by without your moving any closer to planning for or meeting personal goals? Studies have shown that this can create anxiety and stress that may be debilitating and even cause illness. To feel more in charge of your life, look at your revised Personal Garden Calendar to see which things are under your command and which aren't. We can't avoid Must Do factors such as working and dealing with family, or basics like eating and sleeping.

But managing the rest and editing out the nonessential tasks requires a take-charge, disciplined approach.

Beyond carrying out the essential tasks in your daily life, adopting a "less is more" attitude will help you increase your sense of control, as well as your ability to perform at a higher level.

6. Ask yourself: *Am I overcommitted? Do I really have time to work, volunteer on three boards, and be the mother I want to be? Am I doing "drive-bys" for social events because I've accepted two or three invitations for a single evening? Has efficiency supplanted my enjoyment because I'm always focused on accomplishing the next thing?*

7. Is your emotional calendar overbooked? Have you taken on so many psychological responsibilities that you're completely drained? A *New York Times* article noted that over two-thirds of the primary caregivers for aging parents are women. Can your siblings do more to help with this elder care? Have you had a heart-to-heart talk with your husband about sharing parental responsibilities such as supervising homework or bedtime routines or driving children to events on weekends?

8. If you're single, whether you're a parent or not, are you addressing your emotional needs? If you do have children, should you consider joining a single-parent support group for networking opportunities or other coping support? Can you make new friends by pursuing interests such as hiking, yoga, tennis, books, and knitting, perhaps by joining clubs for people with these hobbies? If you're suffering grief due to death or divorce, have you taken proactive steps (getting involved in therapy, a grief group, or counseling) to put these issues on the front burner, address them, and move on?

Tina's Story

Tina's husband was ill for a number of years before he died, leaving her as the primary provider for her two children. She was only 40 years old. The shock of her husband's death was huge, and she was faced with three major emotional issues: her own loss of her spouse, her children's loss of a parent, and being thrust into the role of sole family provider.

For a number of months, Tina suffered from depression and completely lost her sense of direction in life. She couldn't move on because she hadn't dealt with the event. She finally sought counseling, and with the support of her friends, she was able to mend herself and create a life reentry plan. Only after she regained a sense of emotional balance was she able to go back into the workforce.

While her husband was ill, Tina had joined a political campaign as a part-time volunteer in order to have an outlet from the stress of caring for him while also raising two children. She was able to use that background as a springboard into a full-time position leading a trade group in California.

Repotting Your Soul:
Tending Your Spiritual Garden

Gardening is as much about tending the soul as the soil, according to George Ball, CEO of the Atlee Burpee & Co. seed company. Repotters need to care for their spiritual soil, too. No matter what their life stage or age, women today have become acutely aware of the need for meaning and a sense of purpose in their lives. Our interviews with accomplished career women, stay-at-home mothers, and retirees—as well as the large numbers of women from all walks of life who have survived life-altering conditions such as cancer—have confirmed this major trend. To answer the growing need for spiritual guidance, the marketplace has responded with everything from megachurches to pray-as-you-go podcasts for stressed-out commuters to an avalanche of self-help books, tapes, and electronic media.

The most obvious catalysts for women's desire to take stock were the events of September 11, 2001. The sense of fragility they created caused many women to make major changes in how they were living their lives, reviewing everything from where they made their homes to their priorities.

But it's more than the 9/11 effect that's causing women to focus on personal spiritual growth. For some, advances in science and medicine don't provide all the answers, while others feel lost in our fast-paced, secular, technologically driven society. We've found that many of those we've interviewed have a new priority: to move the spiritual component front and center. They're experimenting with many ways to fill this need. It can be as simple as making time for meditation and reflection or as major as leaving a career to attend a seminary.

An increasing number of women find that giving back and helping create better lives for others is a compelling outlet that satisfies their need for a sense of spirituality. Many are putting these activities ahead of entertainment or other self-oriented pursuits. Some are incorporating philanthropic elements into their vacations, looking for ways to give back to the communities they're visiting.

This trend has created a new field called "travel philanthropy," in which people go to places such as Ecuador and Africa to help the underprivileged.

Women are also engaging in personalized spiritual activities (often called "do it yourself" religion), joining an organized religious community, or spending time in nature. Often, something as simple as spending more time with family members helps create the sense of spiritual completeness. You may want to identify a touchstone or important value in *your* inner garden that will motivate you to repot.

We interviewed a number of accomplished career women who came to a point in their lives when they had to ask themselves, *Is this all there is?* In spite of the financial and personal rewards they reaped from their work, these women could no longer ignore their inner voices, which were asking, *What have I really done with my life?*

In one case, Maureen, a public-relations executive, looked at her life and found that in spite of her professional accomplishments, her inner "balance sheet" was deficient—she was in the red. She repotted by selling the business she'd started and brought more light into her life by using her financial resources, time, and talents to mentor at-risk children.

Deborah, another professional, sold her highly successful software company and consciously made the decision to give back. She said, "It's the beginning of a spiritual journey. I ask myself, *What does it mean to be alive? What is my purpose in being here?* I think about it every day."

For Maureen and Deborah, the answer to spiritual fulfillment lay in serving nonprofit community organizations. Melissa and Jane, however, took a religious path that satisfied their spiritual needs. Melissa was a graphic designer who had never lost touch with her faith-filled upbringing. While traveling in Africa on a missionary trip, she contracted malaria and was in danger in the midst of a war-ravaged country. After surviving this trauma, she returned to Washington, D.C., to resume her design work. But as she reflected on her experiences, she chose a spiritual purpose over temporary earthly success, deciding to start a Bible-study group. Fourteen years later, she leads a sizable organization, and the women she's mentored have started satellite groups in surrounding communities. She notes, "I feel complete. If I did anything else, I'd be miserable."

Jane was a homemaker and mother of four. When a member of her church suggested, in the early 1970s, that she study to become a priest, she was shocked by the audacity of the idea. Not only were there very few women in the church hierarchy, but she'd never contemplated such a major commitment to her faith. She took the leap, however, and enrolled in a seminary, was ordained, and became the acting bishop of her diocese. Today, she teaches religion at a local university.

Jane's journey of self-discovery is representative of a broader trend: the increased enrollment of women in mainline divinity schools. Women now make up 51 percent of the students in divinity school, according to a *New York Times* article. Such an education answers many women's need to go deep into themselves and explore what matters to them and what doesn't. Many seminary graduates, including some of our interviewees, are forgoing the pulpit in favor of careers in social advocacy, academia, or in their primary professions.

Exercise: The Soul Scan

Like the women described in the previous section, you may be feeling that your life isn't complete. If career, family, and other accomplishments aren't quite enough for you, perhaps it's time to bring some more spiritual light into your garden. Beautiful blooms don't emerge unless they've been given enough sun.

Start your scan by completing this exercise in your *Repotting 101 Workbook* or using your own materials. Keep your revised Personal Garden Calendar handy.

1. When you review the past weeks' or months' activities, do you feel that some of them created a sense of fulfillment for you? If you're pursuing a career, is it one you feel comfortable with? For instance, are you spending 12 hours a day as a lobbyist for corporate interests when your inner voice tells you that you should be closer to nature, perhaps starting your own business as a florist? If you're a homemaker, do you sometimes feel that some of your energy could be dedicated to helping others in the community? If you're retired, do you sometimes want to reallocate time spent on entertainment (for example, playing bridge, attending shows and lunches, or ballroom dancing) toward some kind of community service?

2. If you want to add a spiritual, religious, or philanthropic component to your life plan, is a lack of time holding you back? If so, you may want to consider making this a priority, revisiting your revised Personal Garden Calendar and editing out other activities to free up space for this important element in your life. (This is part of the "trade-off" test we talked about earlier.)

3. Ask yourself: *If I could replant myself and find more meaning and purpose in my life, what would I change?* Consider what combination of your time, talent, hard work, and money you're willing to dedicate if giving back is your goal. Think about how you'd like to go about this—whether you'd like to get involved in the arts, helping the disadvantaged, global causes (environment, peace, or world hunger), local or national politics, or something else. (See our links in the Resources section to stimulate your thinking.) For some women, simply dedicating more time to their spouse, children, extended family, an aging parent or relative, neighbors, or a friend in need will fulfill their spiritual vacuum.

Exercise: Training to Repot— Conditioning Your Soil

For a gardener, getting the soil in good shape is essential for growing healthy plants. The purpose of this exercise is to get yourself in the best condition possible so that you can repot yourself. It will involve going into training in all three areas of your life: physical, mental, and spiritual. Repotters have to improve their personal soil—their well-being—in order to make their transitions successfully.

For the following exercise, use the appropriate pages in your *Repotting 101 Workbook* or use a blank piece of paper. Divide it into three sections: Physical, Mental, and Spiritual. Each of these sections needs to have two columns: Current and Future. Refer to your revised Personal Garden Calendar (either in your workbook or the one you've created) to review your current time commitments to self-care rituals in these three areas by writing down the amount of time you spend in each category over a one-month period.

Step 1: Your current life. Look at how you're allocating time for each of these three components. In the columns labeled "Current," is there time already allocated on your revised PGC for each of these categories? If not, can you find time, and are you willing to devote the energy to enhance your own well-being? It may not be possible for you to make a large commitment in all three categories at once, so put your energy where your need is the greatest.

Step 2: Your future life. Once you've decided on what you'd like to start doing in each category, jot it down in the columns labeled "Future" and allocate a realistic amount of time to devote to this proposed activity. You may need to make adjustments based upon your availability. For example, you might decide that you'd like to start taking a fitness class at a nearby school, but when you calculate how much time would be involved in getting prepared, traveling, and doing it, you might instead decide that walking your dog is a more efficient way to get in your exercise.

The Conditioning Your Soil chart that you've created will help you take a disciplined approach to bringing more "light" (improved physical, mental, and spiritual well-being) into your life. You're now in a training mode.

> **Personal Gardening Tip:** Previsualize your ideal garden. You need a mind-set that will enable you to put your physical, mental, and spiritual values in the driver's seat. You must set aside time to focus on your needs, create a strategy to meet your goals, and follow through on your plan. You can only imagine your ideal garden when you first visualize the steps you'll need to take in order to create it.

After completing these exercises, you may find that your physical, mental/emotional, and spiritual well-being are at different levels from each other or from where you may want them to be—or that they may even be nonexistent. One area may need more attention than another, or you may need to make changes in a number of places. But to add more light into your garden, you have to start somewhere, even if it's a small effort. Decide if the life you want to lead is one in which you're more physically fit, mentally sharp, and spiritually aware or fulfilled. Whether you're on your way to repotting or about to start your repotting process, you may want to consult the Resources section in the Appendix for more information on bringing your physical, mental, emotional, and spiritual priorities into focus.

In the next chapter, we'll look at how adding nutrients to your personal landscape—in the form of lifelong learning—will position you for successful repotting.

Chapter Four

Do You Need More Fertilizer?

Every gardener knows that adding fertilizer to the soil is essential for the growth and maintenance of her garden. This food for plants plays a key role in replenishing the earth with nutrients and minerals. It's used to strengthen existing specimens, jump-start root growth, and make blossoms flourish. But no single fertilizer is right for all types of soils or species—different mixes work for varying locales and plants. These additives can revitalize a "spent" garden environment and give it new life, promoting a fresh growth cycle.

Women today are fertilizing their lives by continually adding to their skills portfolio as a form of self-enrichment. They now represent nearly 57 percent of all college and university students. Married women (with and without children) and single parents are on campus in record numbers—they comprise 47 percent and 21 percent of college students respectively, according to the American Council on Education. A 2002 report by The National Center for Education Statistics shows that women make up 44 percent of law school students, 30 percent of M.B.A. candidates, 45 percent of students in medical school, and 55 percent of all C.P.A. graduates nationwide. While only 15 percent of engineering candidates are female, this percentage continues to increase. These statistics are evidence of women's strong and growing commitment to lifelong learning.

The fertilization process is both an impetus and a foundation for repotting. Women are using education as a primary garden tool to create a new identity for themselves and develop a new life plan. If you're thinking about repotting, your life may need an injection of nutrients (education) that will enable you to make significant changes by giving you new skills, ideas, inspiration, and direction. You can undertake this enrichment at any point in your life; your capacity to learn and grow never ends. Almost every woman we interviewed had tapped into some form of education program to assist or stimulate her in the repotting process.

Learning can take many shapes, from a formal degree program to a computer class at a local high school, from online research to a workshop in knitting, pottery, or another hobby. All of these types of education provide stimulation and replenish your soil so that you can grow in whatever direction you choose. In some cases, this process is critical for helping you acquire the credentials necessary for repotting into a new life; in other cases, this fertilizer is needed if you want to foster the changed mind-set that is pivotal for new growth. In addition, research shows that as we age, learning new things keeps the mind nimble and protects the brain from dementia and Alzheimer's, among other diseases. Your unique set of life conditions will determine what fertilizer *you* need for the repotting process.

Preparing Your Garden for Fertilization:
Taking an Interests-and-Skills Inventory

Women have many motivating factors that make them pursue enrichment. Later in this chapter, we'll describe two different kinds of learning: personal improvement and career-related knowledge. Whether or not you're already involved in some kind of educational program, this chapter will help you decide whether it's time to expand that pursuit or start something new.

Not everyone knows exactly where to begin or what kind of learning journey they should follow. The exercise below will help you identify areas that you may be interested in. Turn to your revised Personal Garden Calendar in your *Repotting 101 Workbook,* or use a blank page that you'll keep with your Idea File.

Exercise: Finding the Right Fertilizer

1. List your interests. These may range from athletic pursuits to global affairs and cultural issues to family matters. If you need help identifying what interests you, note the subjects you tend to read about regularly in books and newspaper and magazine articles. Look at your bookmarked Websites—what do they have in common? What information-based programs do you watch or listen to? Do you regularly tune in to HGTV (Home & Garden TV) or listen to a health-related radio program?

2. List your skills. Write down the abilities you've developed in every possible area of your life, whether they're experience-based (acquired while doing volunteer work, managing a home, or building a career); talents (athletic, cultural, or organizational); or knowledge-based skills (whether polished while earning a degree or studying more informally).

3. Prioritize this list. Select three interests you want to explore further. Could one of them be a possible cornerstone for your repotting plan? For instance, you may decide that your volunteer work teaching underprivileged children could be the basis for obtaining a degree in early-childhood education. Or, if you want to translate your cooking skills into your own catering business, you may decide to enroll in a local women's business-training center to get the entrepreneurial skills you need. If you notice that you clip a lot of gardening articles, you may decide to join a garden club and begin spending more of your time outdoors.

4. Assess your current skills. Ask yourself whether your present abilities would allow you to pursue your interests to the degree you'd like. If not, perhaps you'll need to enrich your life with additional learning. For instance, if you were a teacher, but have been home raising a family, it's likely that you'll need to renew your certification.

Fertilizing Your Personal Garden: Tending Your Blossoms

Just as a garden is constantly evolving and changing, so, too, is your life. Our research has revealed that personal improvement is a major motivator for those pursuing enrichment. Women are asking, "Do I want to learn something or change something about myself?" Some are focused specifically on their appearance and would like to get a makeover, lose weight, or develop a different wardrobe. Others want or need to improve some aspect of their health and are interested in becoming more fit, quitting smoking, or learning more about nutrition. And many are focused on addressing personality issues, developing better interpersonal and speaking skills, getting life coaching, learning more about etiquette, or simply engaging in general personal growth.

Some repotters want to reconnect with a long-neglected interest. Increasingly, women are becoming involved in interest-based education—classes in cooking, singing, dancing, sports, pottery, and the like—that leads to personal enrichment. Many different Websites offer descriptions of various interests and hobbies and, in some cases, provide information about developing relevant skills, including names and locations of training centers and helpful books and newsletters. They may even offer tests to help you determine what career or pursuit would fit your personality.

For some women, pursuing a hobby is not only a way to discover something new, but also to widen their social network. For instance, joining a knitting or sailing club can help them meet new people. Others become involved in projects that require learning new skills. Home Depot now offers in-store classes on home improvement just for women because so many are taking on renovation projects themselves. In addition, as a respite from the stresses of caregiving or other obligations, women are taking seminars, classes at local community colleges, and online courses.

Jenny's Story

One woman we interviewed discovered her real interest while rearranging her den. Having removed all the books from the shelves, she sorted them by category. She was stunned to discover that one entire side of her den was stacked with books about historic preservation. She suddenly realized that this subject had been a strong interest for most of her adult life. At the same time, she was scaling back from her full-time career as a lawyer and lobbyist. Having come face to face with her longtime fascination with historic preservation, she decided to make it her repotting goal to spend more time being involved in it. She applied to a graduate program in historic preservation at a local university and was accepted. She doesn't know how or if she'll use this degree in a professional endeavor, but the learning experience will provide the personal fulfillment she's seeking.

Finding the Right Fertilizer for You

Not everyone has clearly defined interests to explore, and even if you do, you may want to expand your search beyond what you already know. The Internet is your personal resource and can lead you to new subjects for exploration. You can start looking for enrichment with some basic research. For example, Websites such as **www.findmeahobby.com** supply lists of a wide range of pursuits that you may not have considered, including coin collecting, scuba diving, and poker. Once you've zeroed in on a subject, you can decide if you want to learn more about it.

Several women we interviewed were introduced to new endeavors through television and friends. One was intrigued by a show on fly-fishing and decided to forgo her beach vacation in favor of attending a fly-fishing instructional camp. Now an avid fly fisher, she not only has a new interest, but she also has a new network of friends. Another woman went to the Great Barrier Reef expecting to snorkel, but while she was there, a friend introduced her to scuba diving. This opened up a whole new avenue of water adventure. She became a certified scuba diver and now spends all her vacation time traveling the world to explore this hobby.

Women are driving the trend toward experience-based training. Some take "learning vacations" that turn into full-time preoccupations or even careers. One returned from sailing camp and decided to become a full-time sailing instructor. A significant number of women we interviewed found that equestrian training, from dressage to three-day eventing, answered their need for a new hobby. These are just two examples of a broad selection of learning experiences that enrich women's lives.

The search for activities that are personally fulfilling often stems from a strong desire to carve out personal time. Because women devote so much to the care of family, parents, and pets, they're looking for activities that will provide them with a personal oasis. Singles who are focused on their careers are also seeking to engage in meaningful endeavors, and aging women have an especially strong sense of the passage of time and the need to do something more for themselves.

Nourishing Your Career Garden:
Improving Your Blossoms with Gardening Tools

Women today understand that being productive and knowledgeable on the job means success, which often translates into financial rewards. Both the number of women participating in the workforce and on college campuses has steadily increased in the last ten years. This isn't surprising, given the relationship between education and income. For many, climbing the "learning tree" entails engaging in an ongoing learning process that takes many forms. A wide variety of classes is available to those in different stages of life and in varying circumstances. Whether they're single or married, young or old, economically comfortable or struggling, most women share a common desire for stimulation and fulfillment.

Career Garden Maintenance

Certain professions—such as teaching, nursing, and child care—require continual lifelong learning to update job skills or obtain state-required certification. To keep current, women may attend weekend seminars, night classes, online courses, or executive programs at universities. A child-care provider we interviewed has to be recertified on a routine basis, requiring her to take a course in CPR annually. Another woman used technical school certificate programs to launch two different careers: one as a ferry pilot and the other as a massage therapist. One interviewee wanted to use her passion for painting and turn it into a business in order to the pay the bills. She decided to take a course at a women's business center to gain the required entrepreneurial skills. At home or at your local library or community center, you can use the Internet to research offerings that are relevant to your specific needs.

Growing Your Career Garden

Women realize that in today's competitive environment, getting ahead requires them to continually add new skills to their portfolios. Corporations not only encourage this, they often require employees to take courses to qualify for a promotion. Indeed, many commercial entities, ranging from local businesses to law firms, offer their own internal "universities" to provide training to all levels of employees. Today, one-third of corporate tuition reimbursements now fund online or blended programs (a combination of online and regular classes that the student physically attends), according to a survey conducted by the American Society for Training & Development in 2005.

Staying abreast of new developments in today's fast-paced world makes the ongoing learning process even more important. A woman working in real estate, for instance, needs to be continually on top of information about interest rates, local and national tax laws, changing demographics, and so on if she's going to succeed or advance in her career.

Changing Your Career Garden

In a *Wall Street Journal* article, one 29-year-old woman was quoted as saying, "People are using education to do what they have always wanted to do." The article goes on to state that students are making more radical changes than they did in earlier decades, and more people are switching careers than ever before. We've spoken to a number of women who are in positions that they no longer find rewarding or satisfying. Despite having invested time, energy, and money becoming qualified in a particular field, they now seek to change careers for several reasons. Perhaps they don't like the work itself; they have changing life circumstances (such as starting a family); or their values, priorities, or interests are shifting.

An extreme example of this phenomenon is a trial lawyer who told us that the long hours and unrewarding nature of her work caused her to leave that profession to enter a seminary. Undertaking such a drastic change at any age requires a woman to commit to an entirely new learning focus. Those who are motivated to make major alterations in their life landscape plan may have to go back to school and get a degree in their new field of interest.

Mary's Story

Mary, who had a B.A. in biology, decided after eight years as a lab researcher that she would never meet her financial goals if she continued in her job. After researching professions that offered the potential for high financial reward, she chose to get a degree in computer science.

This decision required her to make a major commitment of time and money. Initially, she had to continue working in the lab in order to pay for night school. After graduating, she became the information technology executive for a major publishing company. She recently retired to the horse farm that her second career enabled her to buy. "Changing course was the best decision I ever made. I never would have been able to live my dream without the income from my second career," Mary told us.

In Mary's case, a second B.A. provided the nutrients she needed in order to repot into a new field. Others contemplating a major career change may require not only an undergraduate education but also an advanced degree, such as an M.A., M.B.A., LL.B., C.P.A., Ph.D., or M.D. Remember that you may need to take certain courses at the undergraduate level as a prerequisite to even enter these higher programs.

Perhaps you're thinking about a change in your life landscape plan because you've decided to make spirituality a priority. An increasing number of universities are offering innovative degree programs for the layperson who wants to integrate faith and work, such as a master's degree in pastoral counseling and spiritual care.

If you're considering leaving one career for another, keep in mind these four factors:

1. Research. You'll need to research your potential new career in depth. Consult the professional organizations associated with it, search the Internet for information, talk to others working in your intended profession, and use any other resources you think are essential for helping you analyze whether you can make the change you desire.

2. Requirements. If you need a new degree in order to change careers, you'll have to research how much it will cost you to earn it. Factor in the time commitment to study and take classes (and travel to and from campus); the monetary costs of tuition, books, and so on; and the impact that working toward a degree will have on your family and lifestyle. Just as you did in Chapter 1, you'll need to decide whether the cost of pursuing the opportunity is one you're willing to pay.

3. Time. Refer to your revised Personal Garden Calendar to figure out how working toward a degree or other qualifications will fit into your new schedule. Do you have the time to make this commitment now? Is this the right point in your life to be pursuing this goal? For instance, if you're paying college tuition for two of your children, can you afford to do so for yourself as well? Or if you're spending most of your free time caring for an aging parent, do you also have the hours available for an enrichment class? If you're married, is your husband (or older children) willing to take on additional responsibilities while you're pursuing your plan? One hallmark of all the successful repotters we've interviewed is their determination to find a way to their goal in spite of major time obstacles.

4. Online. Is it feasible for you to obtain a certificate, degree, or enrichment class online? In the past few years, the number and quality of Web-based offerings has grown enormously—even Harvard and UCLA now grant online degrees. This is good news for women who need to stay in their current job while seeking credentials for a new career.

Christiane's Story

Christiane's story reveals some of the trade-offs involved in committing to a degree program in order to make a career change. After earning a B.A., Chris became a top salesperson in a stock market research company. A single mother supporting two children, she met her second husband on this job. He became her main support system when she decided to go back to school for an M.B.A.

During the first year of this program, she dated and married her husband. Then, in year two, she became pregnant; and finally, in year three, she continued to work and attend class while breast-feeding. Her decision to enter a professional degree program to advance in her career required tremendous sacrifice on her part and by her new husband and family.

Having left her previous job, Chris is now using her M.B.A. skills to work with her older daughter, who has started her own entrepreneurial venture in retail. Chris commented, "I couldn't be of any help to my daughter without this degree program. I feel that I'm passing down a legacy to her and the rest of my family."

Nourishment for Aging Gardens

Just as you can change your garden at any point in time, you can also enhance yourself through learning at any age. Many retirees are choosing urban environments to live in, partly because they want to take advantage of classes offered at nearby universities. Older women who may have deferred a degree due to marriage, childbearing, financial circumstances, or other factors are flocking back to campuses for either enrichment or degree courses. At the age of 55, Jean returned to Columbia University to complete the bachelor's degree she'd started 37 years earlier. Her motivation was to fulfill her own personal desire for an education, and to feel that in conversation, she could intellectually match up with her friends, who had completed their degrees.

Repotting Your Brain Online

We can't talk about the learning process today without highlighting the many opportunities that the Internet offers. It's no longer necessary to be on campus to get an associate, bachelor's, or master's degree—all are offered through online universities. Retirees who can't physically take advantage of campus-based classes now recognize that access to education is one click away. Working mothers and single women can advance themselves or their careers without ever having to leave their homes. Whether your interest is learning more about becoming a therapist or improving your cooking skills, online information can help you start and even provide certification.

The University of Phoenix's online college was at the forefront of moving the classroom from a building to the Internet, and now prestigious institutions such as Harvard and Yale are following suit. For serial repotters who are refueling their brains for yet another career or life pursuit, the Internet offers a 24/7 route to new skills and credentials.

Unexpected Outcomes: Gardening Surprises

Gardeners sometimes plant flowers with one thing in mind and end up with surprising results! In the same way, several of our interviewees started out with one learning goal, only to discover after reaching it that they wanted to modify their original plan. Karen, a successful entrepreneur in the real estate appraisal business, wanted to learn to become a massage therapist as an outlet for her nurturing side. Her original idea was to become a certified masseuse, work as a therapist full-time, and sell her other business. However, once certified, Karen decided that she would be a partial repotter—a woman who determines that a full-scale transformation of her life isn't the right choice for her at the moment. Karen is keeping her real estate company, but works part-time as a massage therapist on weekends. (See Chapter 8 for a more in-depth discussion of Karen's story.)

Meena had been taking art classes as a means of getting out of the house and adding some enrichment to her life. Little did she know that years later, her interest in art and the classes she took would become the foundation for her new business endeavor. Later, when she decided to become a fashion consultant and accessories designer, (drawing on her artistic skills) she took classes in entrepreneurship to help her in her business.

Leslie lost her job in an accounting firm. After sitting at home for six months, she started to paint the walls of her own home with decorative designs out of frustration. Friends and visitors started to ask her if she could do something similar in their own homes. Leslie has now grown her hobby into a full-time business.

> **Personal Gardening Tip:** Fertilize your garden. If repotting is your goal—if you want to change your personal life landscape—you may need to add some type of enrichment to your life.

Repotting your life often requires ongoing learning that can take many forms and cover a wide range of subjects. It's your job to figure out what kind and how much education you need and how often to pursue it in order to facilitate your change. We've found that successful repotters always engage in some form of learning as part of their repotting process.

This is one essential aspect of repotting. Like any other change that you feel you need to make as you redesign your life landscape, going back to school involves some level of uncertainty. If you want to repot, you'll have to determine your tolerance for risk. The next chapter will help you figure out whether you're ready to make a change and leave your current flower bed.

Chapter Five

Have You Outgrown
Your Current Planter?

Whether you're a skilled horticulturist or a novice gardener, at some point you'll probably have to consider moving plants that have outgrown their current space into a new environment—a new container or flower bed. Gardeners hope that if they give their specimens a chance to grow in new terrain, the plants will be revitalized and flourish.

But this transplantation process often involves some risk. The mere removal of a plant may be so traumatic that it dies. In addition, if the new environment isn't right—too much sun or wind, the wrong soil mix, or some other problem—it will languish, and may even wither and perish. Knowing the risks involved in moving the plants, and finding solutions to potential problems before uprooting them, is crucial to a successful transplant.

Changing your environment may mean moving into a new "space"—a different career, lifestyle, or an area of interest, for example. This involves taking risks, some of which may be relatively small, while others may entail, as one of our repotters said, "jumping off the proverbial cliff." Whatever shift you're considering, you'll need to evaluate a number of factors.

To begin, you'll have to assess your "risk mentality": How prepared and willing are you to break out of your flower box and replant yourself? Next, you need to consider how you'll deal with the financial, emotional, time, and status risks you'll take. Finally, you'll analyze the consequences—both positive and negative—if you repot. In this chapter, we've provided exercises that will help you anticipate, manage, and accept the risks involved in your journey.

The "No Boundaries" Mind-set

For many years, women were characterized as being more timid than men—more cautious, risk averse, and afraid of change. While there may have been some truth to this in earlier decades, women in the 21st century are disproving this characterization on a daily basis. From riding motorcycles to climbing Mount Everest, women are going to extremes on all fronts. Danica Patrick, the Indy 500 Rookie of the Year who drove her way into the history books at the Indianapolis 500, and Ellen MacArthur, who sailed solo around the world, are just two examples of today's courageous pioneers. The woman next door who starts a cookie business in her home could become the next "Mrs. Fields" overnight. Throughout the country, in small towns and big cities, women are leaving the safety of their current flower boxes, finding new ground, and repotting themselves.

Moving into broader growth environments for work and pleasure, women are making headway in job arenas such as construction and farming: They now own or co-own about 20 percent of construction firms, according to the *Wall Street Journal,* and are the principal operators of almost 240,000 farms as reported by the 2002 U.S. Census of Agriculture.

They're also filling top administrative posts at universities, once the sole purview of men: Women hold 27 percent of all deanships, including 8 percent of all law school and 3 percent of all medical school deanships. They comprise almost 20 percent of all presidents of colleges and universities in this country, according to an article in *Liberal Education.* Many of them are leading-edge baby boomers, the first group of women to rise to the top of historically male professions.

A *New York Times* article profiled Nance Dicciani, president and chief executive, specialty materials, at Honeywell International. The title of the piece was "No Boundaries Please" and it focused on that phrase as her life's mantra and her mental outlook. The principal of her high school told her to never let anyone set boundaries for her. She followed this advice throughout her life, entering chemical engineering at a time when she was the only woman admitted to the program. Her no-boundaries mind-set enabled Nance to overcome difficult challenges along the way. She has even repotted part of her life by pursuing a pilot's license.

Regardless of what age you are or life stage you're in, and no matter what future you envision for yourself, adopting a "no boundaries" mind-set is crucial for reaching your goal. We've found that each of our repotter interviewees had replaced (or was willing to replace) their fears about change and the unknown with a new, courageous attitude. As Tina, a former tennis pro who became a spa director, said, "I don't let fear stop me on life's journey."

Laureen's Story

Laureen told us, "I always wanted to be a pioneer." She started by challenging gender stereotypes in sports, a pattern she later carried over into her professional career. She went from being the receptionist to her first management position at TVS Television Network, covering NCAA basketball, WFL football, and NASL soccer. In 1982, she continued to break down barriers and flourish in the television sports landscape by helping launch SportsVision in Chicago, one of the first regional sports networks in the country, serving as both the only woman and only Asian-American in sports-franchise management. As one of the first women in this industry, she also didn't have the help of other women to mentor her along the way and relied on her own skills and courageous attitude.

During her 30 years in television, Laureen has worked in just about every part of the business—ad sales, syndication, news, sports, local-affiliate broadcasting, and cable—tackling every kind of job and building on her previous experience. She's always embraced risks, including financial ones, such as when she managed syndication sales for MTM distribution, where her salary was based on her sales record. For two years, she was vice president and general manager of WTTG in Washington, D.C., one of Fox Broadcasting's largest and most successful television stations, where she was the first (and possibly only) Asian-American woman to lead a top-ten-market affiliate.

Most recently, she served as president of the National Geographic Channel (NGC). She held the position prior to the launch of the channel, and in first five years on the job, she led the network as it increased its distribution from 10 million to more than 60 million households across the U.S. In honor of her career and success with NGC, Laureen was recognized in November 2005 as the "Woman of the Year" by the Women in Cable Telecommunications (WICT).

She said, "Many times I chose the road less traveled . . . and many of those choices were tough. But each one came with individual rewards." She added, "But what has been a key to my success . . . was my ability to manage, face, and ultimately overcome any challenge."

Going to Extremes

Women's "no boundaries" mind-set goes beyond the workplace. The number of females in extreme sports such as long-distance running and rock climbing has grown significantly in the last 20 years as they challenge themselves physically. They made up a growing percentage of the almost 300,000 people who participated in any triathlon in 2005, according to a *New York Times* article.

Pam Reed is representative of this attitude. She's the two-time reigning champion of Badwater, the 135-mile race from California's Death Valley to Mount Whitney that's considered the world's toughest running event. In addition, she's the first person on record—male or female—to run 300 miles straight without sleep. Pam has completed more than 100 races exceeding marathon distance, including 20 races of 100 miles or more.

Several of the women we interviewed have taken their mental focus from the workplace to extreme sports such as backcountry skiing, three-day horse eventing, and ice climbing. Female Olympians have set new world records and are closing the performance gap with men in many athletic endeavors. In addition, women-only adventure travel has risen 40 percent in the last 10 years, another indicator of women's interest in challenge.

Many of today's women have embraced risk in their lives, viewing it as positive and stimulating rather than frightening or intimidating. As one interviewee told us, those who have been high achievers in the corporate world seek out other endeavors that entail similar dangers and goal setting. But not everyone is ready or willing to undertake this kind of challenge; fear can hold many women back.

Fear Factor

What's your greatest fear about repotting? Do you find change at any level threatening? Some of our interviewees were paralyzed at the very thought of uprooting themselves and establishing a new norm. Women are often reluctant to give up the status quo.

But maybe your biggest worries have to do with finances. Are you so emotionally tied to your regular paycheck that you can't allow yourself to experiment with a different financial equation? Are you so invested in the status associated with your paying job that you can't contemplate giving it up in favor of a more satisfying endeavor?

The financial risks of leaving a job are real. Even when women repot themselves by abandoning their jobs temporarily, it can prove costly. On average, women who leave work for only 2.2 years and return after that time lose an average of 18 percent of their earning power when they go back. This figure rises to a staggering 37 percent when they leave for three or more years, as noted in the *Inc.* magazine article, "The Persistent Glass Ceiling."

Cultural barriers may also inhibit a woman's willingness to take risks to reinvent herself. Many Hispanic and Asian women, for instance, are the first in their families to work toward a college degree (or beyond), and often have to overcome resistance from spouses and parents. For some, the barriers include their culture's disapproval of women working outside the home. These are just a few of the reasons that women feel fearful about making a major life change.

Rosa's Story

Rosa came to the United States from Ecuador with a bachelor's degree. She'd left behind three children and an ex-husband, hoping to start a better life in America. Due to the language barrier and her immigrant status, she had to start over from scratch, working as a cook, housekeeper, babysitter, and house manager. She finally saved enough money to buy a home in Maryland and bring her three children there to live with her.

Her first leap into the unknown was leaving Ecuador for the United States. Her second jump took her from her job as a paid house manager to a new role as an entrepreneur and owner of a community bodega, a small grocery store specializing in South American products and cuisine. To accomplish this feat, she had to add to her skills set by taking classes in business ownership at a local women's business center.

"I'm a curious person and a risk taker," said Rosa. "I found that no matter what sacrifices I've had to make, I've been able to keep the goals of independence and a better life in front of me." She credits her ability to reinvent herself in so many different ways to her persistence and her ability to take risks. Looking to the future, she may want to open a restaurant or night club, relying on her "no boundaries" mind-set to reach this goal.

Exercise: Are You Ready to Leave Your Flower Box?

You may be panicking about what might happen if you change your life. Or you could feel as if you're trapped in a swamp and are immobilized by the thought of striking out on your own. This exercise will help you determine if you're ready to analyze the real—not imagined—risks associated with repotting.

Answer the following questions in your *Repotting 101 Workbook,* or use your own materials.

1. Do you feel comfortable with the idea of change—major or small—in your life?

2. Do you feel that risk can be stimulating, energizing, and desirable?

3. Do you feel an increase in your stress level when you think about taking the chances involved in making changes?

4. If you were faced with an opportunity to make a significant alteration in your life recently, did you take advantage of it?

5. Do you put your own needs last when considering a shift in your life?

6. Do you allow factors beyond your own interests to determine how you feel about change? For instance, would you avoid making a switch based primarily on the views of your peers, family, or community?

7. Do you feel unable to act when faced with the prospect of an unknown outcome?

8. Do you tend to use your perceived limitations as excuses for not making a change?

9. Do you actively seek out different experiences on a regular basis? For example, are you the trip planner in your family or the person who suggests, "Let's do something new tonight"?

10. As you look forward to the next ten years in your life: A) Do you feel that you'll be happier if you continue on your present course? Or, B) Are you interested in trying to create a new identity for yourself, even if it means attempting something unknown?

Give yourself one point if you answered *Yes* to questions 3, 5, 6, 7, 8 and 10A and zero points if you answered *No*. Give yourself one point for answering *No* to questions 1, 2, 4, 9, and 10B and zero for answering *Yes*. The higher your score, the more risk averse you are.

If you have a score of five or more, you'll need to look at your current mind-set and work on your risk tolerance, because all repotting involves change. To start and successfully complete the process, you have to feel positive about the modifications you need to make.

Like some of our interviewees, you may be a candidate for partial repotting, where you can start small, trying out your idea without major disruption or risk to your current life (see Chapter 8 for more on partial repotting). Programs such as Outward Bound and similar individual growth organizations can be useful in helping you increase your self-confidence and assertiveness. Please refer to page 247 for more resources.

Leaving the Flower Box: Analyzing Real-World Risks

As gardeners view the layout of their landscape, they're constantly weighing the consequences of moving plants from one part of the garden to another, and assessing the impact that any new additions may have. They need to look at each individual change and assess the risks posed by changing conditions such as wind, sun, water, and surrounding plants. Once they've decided that the change is worth the risk, it's time to take the next step.

Like gardeners, repotters must gauge the hazards and consequences as they envision a new life landscape. Having gone through this process ourselves, we're not underestimating the significance of the many challenges you'll face when redesigning your life. Among the real-world risks are changes in finances, emotions, and time commitments. Your status may be affected by shifts in your job title and identity, resulting in different opinions from your peers. Your family hierarchy can also be in flux if, for example, you go from being a wage earner to a noncontributory status.

Almost all of our repotters had to grapple with at least one of these challenges and referred to the prospect and process of change as "scary" and "hard work." Like them, you need to assess these risks in order to move forward with your repotting process in a realistic way. Having evaluated your outlook in the preceding exercise, you now need to look at the specific risks that may be facing you.

In each of the next four sections, please read the questions pertaining to finances, status, emotional risk, and time. (You can also find them in your *Repotting 101 Workbook*.) The purpose of these exercises is to get you to start thinking about your ability to recognize the challenges associated with your plan and determine your willingness to handle the consequences of making a change.

The Money Tree

We understand that for every woman—single, married, aging, or just out of college—financial considerations are a critical part of making the decision to repot. Transplanting your life may require a temporary interruption in income in anticipation of greater returns later. For instance, a woman who wants to start her own business may be leaving the security of a steady paycheck in favor of potentially greater rewards from an entrepreneurial venture.

On the other hand, a woman who isn't currently generating income for the family, but decides to go back to school, may have to drain her savings or take out a loan to pay for her education, knowing that eventually she'll be able to earn enough to replenish her savings or pay back the loan. For retirees or those on a fixed income, developing a hobby or interest may mean reallocating funds or other financial sacrifices. But with risk often comes reward. One repotter, who gave up her corporate law practice to become a college sailing coach and pursue her passion for writing, said about her loss of income, "I may be poor financially, but I am rich as a person."

No matter what change you're considering, there will probably be a financial impact on you or your family. The questions that follow are designed to help you focus on some of the fiscal risks.

Exercise: Where Are You on the Money Tree?

- If you're single, how do you support yourself (salary, parents, inheritance, savings, annuities, investments, other)?

- If you're a single mother, are you the sole provider for your family?

- If you're married, do you make a financial contribution to your family budget? What's the percentage of your contribution—most of the funds, a small percentage, or none?

- Are you on a fixed income?

Exercise: Weighing the Financial Risks of Change

- How dependent are you or your family on your current income?

- Are you willing to give this up—in whole or in part, temporarily or permanently—if it's necessary to reach your repotting goal?

- Can you or your family survive a reduction or elimination of your monetary contribution—temporarily or permanently?

- Have you discussed with relevant family members the potential financial impact of making a change? For instance, will your husband have to work longer hours? Will your children have to forgo summer camp or make other sacrifices? Will your parents have to cover the gap in your income?

- Is your self-image affected by the amount of money you earn? If you give up a well-paid job for a more meaningful position that provides a lower income, how will you feel about yourself?

- If you reduce your fiscal contribution to the family or stop contributing to it altogether, how will your sense of self-worth be affected?

- How willing are you to make sacrifices (such as having less disposable income, less overall free time and time with family, or fewer leisure activities) in order to meet the financial requirements of your repotting process?

The Status Issue

For many women, entering the workplace has resulted not only in increased income, but also an increased sense of self-worth due to their pride in having a job and a title to go with it. After working so hard and making innumerable sacrifices to get a place on the ladder—whether it's in the corporate world or elsewhere—some may now be reluctant to give up this hard-earned reward. As women contemplate change, the issues around their position and status take on great significance, and they may have difficulty letting go of the prestige they have earned. Indeed, self-image can be rooted so deeply in career, title, and income that many women today can't envision themselves without them.

One of our repotters, Carol, climbed the ladder of magazine publishing and then founded her own magazine. Her passion for horses motivated her to sell her business so that she could spend more time on her hobby. But she had to ask herself, *Who am I if I'm not the publisher of this magazine?* Whether you're running an organization and have the title of CEO or you're teaching kindergarten, the psychic investment you have in your work presents an enormous obstacle to change. Coming to terms with a life that doesn't include an easily recognized label is central to your risk assessment process. This is particularly true of women who've achieved great success. As Carol said, "It's the fact that we're successful that makes change difficult." Answer the questions in the next exercise to see how invested you are in your current identity.

Exercise: Examining Status Issues

1. If you don't work currently, how invested are you in your role as a homemaker, a volunteer, or "CEO" of your family?

2. Can you handle not being at the helm at home if your new identity requires you to delegate domestic responsibilities to your spouse or to hire someone else to run the home front?

3. Will you feel guilty turning over primary responsibility for your children to a caregiver if your repotting plan requires it?

4. If you don't currently bring home a paycheck, how will your husband feel if you start to work outside the home?

5. If you do have a formal job at the moment, how invested are you in your title? Can you feel confident in who you are if you don't have it?

6. How do you think your peers will react to you without a title or your current identity?

7. How will your family view you if you change your identity, title, and so on?

8. How will you react to giving up your place in your community in favor of a different lifestyle, work, or pursuit?

9. Can you work happily on your own, or do you need the support and recognition you get in an office environment?

10. Can you tolerate losing contact with colleagues in your current endeavor if that's necessary for you to pursue your new one?

11. Will you and your spouse be able to handle the change in the dynamics of your relationship if you stop contributing to family finances?

12. How will you feel about yourself if you're not regularly contributing to the family bank accounts?

13. Will you be comfortable if your repotting means that your husband, children, or peers feel a twinge of resentment, or alter their view of you?

14. If you decide to give up a high-level position for a philanthropic pursuit, will your sense of giving back be enough for you, or will you need to assume a management position to feel validated?

Emotional Risks

While financial and status issues are largely quantifiable and tangible, your emotional response to change may be less easy to predict. On paper, your personal landscape plan may look logical, predictable, and feasible. In reality, it's impossible to anticipate all the scenarios that could emerge, much less your reaction to them. This process is full of surprises and uncertainties that even the most experienced repotter can't predict.

When thinking about change, our interviewees have experienced emotional turmoil through periods of success and failure. They've said that the ability to tolerate emotional risk has been crucial to their successful transplanting. A woman named Hilary noted, "After 25 years off campus, I entered a master's degree program at a local university. I felt as if everyone in the class had to be much smarter than me. How could I possibly handle the pressure?" The following questions will help you start exploring some of the emotional risks associated with the repotting process.

Exercise: Assessing Emotional Risks

1. Can you emotionally handle major changes and the instability that accompanies them if you choose to repot?

2. Can you manage the uncertainty of unknown outcomes caused by your decision?

3. Many life changes, such as starting a new business, involve rejection and failure. Can you cope with these risks?

4. Are you willing to deal with any new sources of stress in your life caused by making changes?

For instance, if you're returning to work, can you take the organizational stress of carpooling and getting to your job on time, as well as feeling the need to be home to cook dinner?

5. Are you willing to start at the bottom of the ladder again? For instance, if you enter a new field, can you handle being a beginner? If you go back to school as a mature adult, how will you feel in a classroom full of 20-year-olds?

6. Will you be able to juggle a new set of circumstances, such as relating to colleagues in your work environment, if you've been an at-home mom?

Time

In earlier chapters, we addressed the key issues facing all women today: time and how to manage it, use it, and create more of it. We've focused on your need to take a realistic look at how you're actually spending your days and then devise ways to put spare hours you create by editing your life in a personal Time Savings Bank. One of the major obstacles to success appears when you're not willing to invest the time necessary to envision, plan, and launch your redesigned life.

Repotting may require you to schedule yourself completely differently, spending more or less time with family, at home, or engaging in leisure activities or outside interests. Successful repotters have told us that their mental commitment to making room for the process has been critical. To deal with the risks you'll have to take, you'll need to adopt a "time commitment" mind-set, accepting that you'll have to make changes in this area.

Sometimes, however, even the best plans can go awry. One repotter we interviewed, who'd started a business with another woman, commented, "I went into this knowing that I was probably going to work harder than my partner would, but I never expected her to want out after less than 11 months. . . . That left me in a huge lurch. The separation took me away from my family, both physically because I was working more hours, and emotionally, because I was consumed and just unavailable to them most of the time."

In spite of this interruption, the repotter's advice to others who find themselves in a similar, unexpected situation, is: "Remember that this [situation] will be over soon. It might cost you more than you expected and it might take longer than it should, but you will go back to being a good spouse and parent . . . soon."

Take a look at your revised Personal Garden Calendar and zero in on the time you spend on the daily essentials of your life. Then, if you haven't already done so, calculate how much you've saved and note it in your personal Time Savings Bank.

By answering the following questions, you'll find out whether you have enough time to repot.

Exercise: Assessing Time Considerations

1. Do you feel comfortable with the amount of time you've allocated for attending to the essential tasks in your life and the extra effort required for your repotting process?

2. If you have some idea about how you want to repot—whether it's a partial or full transplant—do you feel that you've accurately estimated how much time you need for the process, and does this allotment fit into your revised Personal Garden Calendar? If not, now would be a good time to revisit the issues raised in Chapters 1 and 2.

3. Are you mentally ready to deal with the unexpected situations that may arise due to your repotting, given that you may have a tighter schedule? For instance, if you leave your full-time job as homemaker to play a management role in a local charitable organization, what happens when a crisis occurs, requiring you to take charge of it, and you're unable to fulfill your obligations at home? Over time, these kinds of conflicts can erode the success of your repotting effort if you haven't anticipated them.

4. Are your mind-set and life flexible enough so that if you fail to achieve your goal, you can deal with the amount of time you've already committed and spent in making this change? For instance, what if you're a single professional woman who decides to repot into an entrepreneurial venture that doesn't work out? Have you thought through your options if your transplant doesn't take?

5. Does your new life landscape plan take into account what will happen if your repotting makes you unable to address your other priorities? Do you believe you'll have enough time to deal with unexpected developments?

> **Personal Gardening Tip:** Change means taking risks. To move forward with the redesign of your personal landscape, you'll have to root out the garden weeds—in other words, face the risks involved in making a life change and overcome them.

You're probably familiar with the saying "No risk, no reward." That was never more true than for women who are redesigning their lives. Calculating the hazards involved in repotting will require careful self-assessment and a realistic appreciation of the kinds of real-world uncertainties described in this chapter. But once you've determined that you share a "no boundaries" mind-set with other 21st-century women who are imagining new lives for themselves, you can let go of your fears, plant your new garden, and watch it grow into something fulfilling and beautiful.

Moving Forward: How to Repot

Part I of this book was designed to help you decide if you're ready to repot. In working through the exercises in Chapters 1 through 5, you've carefully assessed your life and mind-set and evaluated your readiness to dig deep and begin the challenge of repotting. You may have come to the conclusion that you need to create more time for yourself before you can move ahead with your life redesign, or you may have decided you need to work on expanding your skills first.

But even if you do need to pause before going forward, we encourage you to join those repotters who now feel they have the right set of gardening tools—mental, emotional, and physical—and read on! Part II will help you explore your values, and provide you with a "how to" manual that will start you on your way toward developing a specific landscape plan that will allow you to create a life that's more meaningful to you.

How Do You Repot?

Prune Your "Instant Garden" Mind-set:
Gardening for the Long Term

To successfully make over a garden, you must start with a plan. *Southern Living* magazine's garden writer noted, "Most successful gardens begin with careful planning. This doesn't mean you must complete it all at once, but it does present a clear path to your goal." Experts estimate that in creating real gardens, you'll spend three times longer dealing with soil, fertilizers, and other enhancements than tending the actual plants. Similarly, the founder of the Behnke Nurseries Co. in Beltsville, Maryland advised, "For a $1 plant, dig a $3 hole." As you learned in Chapters 1 through 5, you need to be fully prepared before you begin to develop and launch your repotting strategy.

Amateur gardeners may operate under the assumption that once they've put seeds in the ground, the tough part is over, but they're wrong—the work has just begun. Gardening requires a commitment mind-set. As a Washington, D.C., plant expert noted, "We tend to think that nature takes care of everything. Maybe that's true out in the wild, but when a . . . [woman] plants, she has to take care of everything. . . . It's not a fast-food thing." Many time-pressed contemporary gardeners are almost pathologically impatient—they want a magic garden that's going to bloom instantly and not need tending. Just look at the QVC channel's offering of a "magic carpet roll"—a mat of seeds that's ready to be placed in your garden and watered, yielding instant blooms. Today's time-starved consumers, mainly women, bought 15,000 of them in 30 minutes.

There's really no such thing as an instant garden—or an immediate life change. In Part I, you worked through many exercises to create time and space for your new venture and to start to add light and fertilizer into your life. At this point, you have to recognize that if you want more meaning in your life, you're going to have to transform it. If your current situation isn't working, you'll have to dig it up and throw it out—in whole or in part. Having completed your repotting readiness training, you're now prepared to initiate the planning phase of redesigning your life landscape.

Gardens and life are living laboratories, not museums. In truth, they're often the end result of decades of trial and error. Our personal "compost piles" are filled with the mistakes we've made along our road to self-definition. But remember, self-forgiveness is as integral to gardening as it is to your attempt to transform your life. But what are gardeners—and repotters—if not optimistic? Many women have done this successfully, and so can you!

Great gardens depend on more than plants; they also require structure to give them form and dimension. As you begin to plan the makeover of your personal garden, you'll need to bring the kaleidoscope of your life into sharper focus. The next chapter will help you look at your current values and touchstones and decide how they can provide a framework for your new life landscape plan.

Chapter Six

Identifying Your Personal Touchstone

Looking at Life Through a Kaleidoscope

Successful repotters have found that they need to be proactive, not reactive, in planning a redesigned life. The world today offers so many options, opportunities, challenges, and experiences at such an accelerated pace that it's easy to live your schedule instead of your life. A central tenet of repotting is setting priorities based on your values so that the choices you make reflect the kind of meaningful existence you are seeking.

Women today are looking through a kaleidoscope. As they deal with changing priorities—a promotion, the birth of a child, or a rekindled interest in a specific talent or hobby—some things come into focus while others become blurred and no longer receive total attention. As women turn the base of the kaleidoscope, the pattern changes, with new shapes becoming more sharply defined. They're blending their needs, wants, and Have To's into an integrated lifestyle that offers fulfillment over time, although not necessarily on a day-to-day basis.

We know that you're in continual flux, and that you're often making adjustments of all kinds. Nevertheless, planning for a redesigned life requires a thoughtful assessment of whether your core values and priorities are in sync with your activities.

What do we mean by "core values"? In the past 15 years, we've listened to women from all walks of life in our focus groups and interviews. The overwhelming majority of them share a group of priorities that shape their lives. The top-10 list below reflects this research but is by no means all-inclusive. When you do the "Values Orbit" exercise in this chapter, feel free to add to the list anything that you feel is crucial to your life.

Top 10 Values of Repotters

1. **Family and Relationships:** Immediate and extended, including grandparents; romantic partners, friends, colleagues, and acquaintances; pets, in one's home or in a barn

2. **Career/Work:** Full-time or part-time, salaried or entrepreneurial, profit or nonprofit

3. **Health:** Overall well-being, including nutrition and emotional, mental, and spiritual wellness

4. **Fitness:** Exercise regimen and sports

5. **Finances:** Salary, savings, and investments

6. **Spirituality:** Organized or "do-it-yourself" worship, daily meditation, yoga, and getting out into nature

7. **Education:** Degree, nondegree, certificate, and enrichment

8. **Travel:** Leisure, educational, and philanthropic

9. **Hobbies/Interests:** Artistic, community-based, and personally fulfilling

10. **Philanthropy:** Volunteering time, donating money or goods, and lending one's talents

The Values Orbit

Imagine yourself at the center of your own solar system. If you're the "sun," so to speak, the planets are your values in orbit around you. At any given time, the most important ones will be closest to you, in the Mercury, Venus, and Earth orbits. Those of lesser importance at this point in time will be in the Mars, Jupiter, Saturn, and outer planets' positions, circling you at the farthest edges of your solar system.

Recognize that some of your values may actually be in the outer orbits, even though you want them to be a priority, because you've been unable to focus on them for a variety of reasons. For instance, you may want to travel and see the world, but family responsibilities or finances are keeping you close to home. Or you may feel that there's something missing in your life, such as a spiritual component, but you haven't yet found a way to include it in your daily or monthly schedule. The purpose of the following exercise is to show you in black and white whether the life you're living is truly the one you want to lead.

SAMPLE VALUES ORBIT

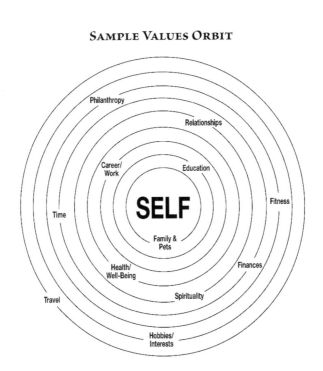

Philanthropy

Relationships

Career/Work

Education

SELF

Fitness

Time

Family & Pets

Health/Well-Being

Finances

Spirituality

Travel

Hobbies/Interests

Exercise: Draw Your Values Orbit

For these three steps, refer to the Values Orbit section of your *Repotting 101 Workbook* or use your own materials (you'll need several pieces of unlined paper).

Step 1: To construct your current Values Orbit, take a piece of plain paper and draw yourself as the sun in the middle, with 10 other concentric circles around you representing the planets. Look at the list of top-10 values on pages 104 and 105. Decide which ones are most important to you at this time and write them into the Mercury position.

You may have more than one value in each ring. For instance, you may feel that relationships, career, and finances are of equal importance; if so, place them all in the Mercury orbit. Write your lesser priorities into the other orbits. If you have a value or priority not on our top-10 list, now is the time to place it on your chart where it belongs. In addition, your Values Orbit may not contain everything in our top-10 list. That's okay—remember, this is *your* life.

Once you've completed the diagram of your current Values Orbit, set aside time to consider whether this values hierarchy accurately reflects how you want your life to look. For instance, maybe "giving back" corresponds with Pluto, but you've been thinking about your affluent and self-oriented lifestyle and feeling uneasy about the lack of time you're devoting to others. You may need to investigate how to move the philanthropic value at least as close to the sun as the Earth orbit.

Or perhaps your family, which you've placed in an outer ring, has been shortchanged because you've been working long hours and traveling for work. Assuming that family time is important to you, you may need to evaluate what steps you have to take in order to move this category into an inner orbit. Do you need to find a new job, or is there some other solution?

It's important to invest time and effort into analyzing your current Values Orbit and to be completely honest with yourself. Without this self-evaluation, you can't create a clear plan for your new garden landscape.

Step 2: Take a second piece of plain paper and draw a second solar system. Again, you're in the center, in the sun position. Now it's time to visualize the life you truly want. In this case, you'll place the values from the top-10 list (and any others of your choice) in orbits according to where you'd *like* them to be.

We realize that this plan for your new Values Orbit isn't going to become a reality overnight. We suggest that you do this exercise several times over the course of a month or more—whatever period of time it takes for you to feel comfortable that the organization of the values on your diagram reflects the life you desire. For example, we know that it will take time and hard work for you to move fitness front and center in your life, if that's what you've decided is important to you. But the very first step is committing yourself to this newly acknowledged goal. Just as there are no instant gardens, there's no shortcut to a new Values Orbit. In coming chapters, we'll help you create the base plan (as landscape designers call it), and plant the life garden that will match your desired priorities.

Step 3: Revisit your Values Orbit diagrams, comparing your current one and your revised version. Look at what you've placed in the orbits closest to you in the second (or future) version. Has it occurred to you that one of these may represent a touchstone—your innermost passion—that will reveal hidden desires in your life? Now that you've done this exercise, have you finally uncovered and brought to the surface a passion that you've allowed to lie fallow but now want to cultivate?

One repotter was surprised by the results of doing this exercise. She told us that crocheting had been an interest and love of hers since her teen years, when her grandmother taught her this art. Recognizing the great satisfaction she derived from her hobby, she moved it from the outer reaches of her solar system to the Venus orbit (the second ring) around her "sun." She'd never had—or made—the time to pursue this passion, but realized that she wanted it back in her life, front and center.

In addition, she loved it so much that she was motivated to start a crocheting business from her home and now sells her handicrafts at local hospitals and nursing homes. Just as it did for this woman, this exercise may unleash the hidden blossoms—or desires—in your life and put you in touch with a motivating passion that will help you determine how you'll repot your life.

The following three stories feature repotters who illustrate the striking transformation that occurs when women are able to identify their inner touchstone or passion and live their lives according to a new Values Orbit.

Nancy's Story: Circling Back to Cultivate a Talent

For Nancy, art has been a "beach ball" that keeps bouncing back at her. As a child, she was more interested in painting a ceramic cat than she was in riding her bike. Taking a cue from her dad, whose hobbies were watercolors and oil painting, she discovered early on that painting was her first love. Although she wanted to major in art in college, her mother advised her to choose a "practical" course of study that would provide her with a job and a steady income. Her mom told her: "You can make art or make a living, but you can't do both."

Over the next ten years, Nancy pursued art history, acquiring a master's degree and a Ph.D., along with teaching credentials. Even while serving in the Peace Corps in South America, she incorporated art into her life by teaching design to the local villagers. Upon her return to the U.S., she taught at Wayne State University in Michigan. While there, she met and married her husband. They settled in Ithaca, New York, where he lived and worked, and started a family.

Her need to be creative continued throughout this period. During the following eight years, Nancy painted and wrote and illustrated children's books. Although they were never published, these books provided an outlet for her passion for art. She also created a home studio, where she worked during summer vacations when she had the most time. In addition, she exhibited her art in local galleries where she and her family vacationed.

The summer shows weren't enough to feed her passion—or meet her financial needs. As a result, in 1994, when her boys were 11 and 13 years old, Nancy reentered the workforce, teaching non-Western and pre-Columbian art at a nearby college. For the next ten years, she taught art history at the same time that she was creating a personal portfolio in her home studio. She even took courses to retrain herself in certain techniques. She'd reached a watershed moment: Should she continue to teach while painting as a hobby, or should she find a way to turn her passion into a full-time career?

From an artistic standpoint, Nancy's first step was to recognize that if she were going to make painting her life, she needed to have her own artistic niche. She reviewed her portfolio and identified her watercolor weavings as a unique body of work that could be potentially lucrative. She set to work refining her unique creativity.

Still unsure about how to turn this work into a paying career, Nancy used her network and talked to other artists about how to convert her talent into a profitable endeavor. She met with a business instructor at the National Women's Business Center, who was an artist involved in marketing and selling her own work. After meeting with encouraging mentors and armed with the beginnings of a business plan, Nancy returned to Ithaca fully committed to making her passion for painting a full-time career. After 25 years of putting art in the Pluto orbit, she was now ready to create a new Values Orbit in which painting, the touchstone of her life, was in an orbit closer to the sun.

This process took several years, and required Nancy to evaluate a number of issues.

1. She had to make a realistic assessment of her own talent and the marketability of her art.

2. She had to determine whether she'd be able to sustain—and preferably increase—her financial contribution to the family if she pursued art full-time.

3. Throughout this process, she had to overcome the preconceived notion, planted in her mind 25 years earlier by her mother, that art wasn't a viable way to make a living.

In this process, Nancy recognized that she'd diminished the value of her gift as well, because she'd been unable to identify the direct benefits of art for others. With her new Values Orbit and mind-set, Nancy saw that by creating artistic beauty, she'd be able to bring enjoyment into her own life *and* the lives of others.

Since 2000, Nancy has been painting full-time, showing her works in exhibits and galleries around the country. She's become a successful artist whose work has been featured in a number of publications, including *Coastal Living* magazine. With the price of her works continuing to rise, she hired consultants this year to revise her business plan. She launched her own Website, is working on a second one, and has expanded her products beyond paintings into prints and note cards.

What's next? Anything's possible. Indeed, Nancy and her husband, a college professor, have considered leaving Ithaca to relocate to the Southwest. How that would influence her art remains to be seen. She told us that her advice to repotters is to follow their dreams, look carefully at their talents, and not ignore their long-held passions—even if they seem to be an unlikely catalyst for the reinvention process. To find your own touchstone, you may have to circle back through your life to identify a pursuit you no longer engage in that made you feel complete or happy, and then go for it!

How else can you learn from Nancy's experience to help your own repotting process? To find your touchstone, you may need to dig deep—even back to a childhood interest. Beyond that, you need to identify the best way to bring that value or interest into your life. For Nancy, painting was her passion, but she also had a strong work ethic. She needed to find a way to combine her creativity with her drive for accomplishment. In spite of life's detours, she found a way to make her Values Orbit reflect her true interests.

Alice's Story: Circling Back to Find a Passion

Alice grew up in Montana, the daughter of two parents who worked in academia. Her childhood was filled with big skies, lots of animals, and the freedom to roam. She graduated from the University of Montana with a degree in clinical psychology—a field that she fell into with a push from her parents.

When she realized that she didn't want a career in that field, she immediately latched onto her interest in cooking as a launchpad for a different career path. She moved to Washington, D.C., and, needing chef credentials, enrolled in and graduated from L'Academie de Cuisine with a degree in pastries. With her newfound skill, she took a job with a local caterer, where she stayed for four years. Alice told us, "The appeal of the kitchen lessened when cooking became work. I was tired of the long hours and being on my feet all day, but mostly, I didn't enjoy working for someone else."

Her dissatisfaction with her chosen career path brought her to a watershed moment. She examined her life to determine what she cared for most in the world. The answer was that she cherished freedom and independence and loved animals. Looking at her Values Orbit, Alice knew that she had to incorporate at least one of those values in her life landscape plan. After conducting research, she decided to train and work as a veterinarian technician. This allowed her to reconnect with a key touchstone—her love of animals—but the low salary and lack of independence at work were two of the drawbacks to this job. Then too, Alice, a single woman, was restless and felt a strong urge to go out on her own and become an entrepreneur.

Her next step was to confirm to herself that she was ready to face the risks involved in starting her own business: the lack of a steady paycheck, the possibility of failure, and the difficulty of managing a new venture without specific business training. Once she decided that she was willing to take these risks, she was ready to identify the kind of company she wanted to start.

In the late 1980s, pet-sitting services were beginning to crop up as more and more women—the primary animal caretakers in their families—were moving into the workplace. Researching the local marketplace, Alice saw an opening for a pet-walking/pet-sitting business catering to busy professionals in Washington, D.C. Sensing a great opportunity, she decided to jump right in. Her mother loaned her the start-up funds, and she began staffing the venture with friends and neighbors who liked the flexible hours and shared her love of animals.

In her start-up phase, Alice faced a number of typical problems. At first, she was overwhelmed with the 24/7 aspects of office management. Hiring competent people was her biggest challenge, especially since her clients' pets and homes were in her care. After the first two years, she'd solved a number of these initial challenges. She hired an office manager and began to find staff by word of mouth.

Alice told us, "Self-employment is a joy. I'm in control of my own life. It's hard work, but I've managed to combine my love of animals with my desire to manage my own time. I feel lucky to be able to combine my passion with my work."

Today, her business is so successful she feels "semiretired." She spends one-third of her time running the business and another third volunteering at the Washington Animal Welfare League, and she still has time to enjoy life. Her interests are leading her down other new paths as well. She's collaborating with an illustrator friend on some children's books featuring animal characters. In the future, Alice hopes to combine her culinary background with animals by creating a new pet food, and she may even write about her experiences over the years.

She recently sold her pet-sitting business and moved to Oregon to pursue new interests.

This story illustrates the importance of making proactive decisions when it comes to rearranging your Values Orbit. Alice could have stayed in the catering field, made pastries, and even started a business in that area. But by carefully examining her life to decide what she loved most in the world, she reconnected with her core value: her love of animals. Once she recognized that she wanted them to be her focal point, she moved them into her inner orbit, while also putting independence in the same position.

C. L.'s Story: Blossoming Where You're Transplanted, Finding Surprises in Your Personal Garden

One of our successful repotters, C. L., told us she feels that women need to look at their entire past to find what captured and motivated them earlier in their life. For her, it was a love of plants, gardening, and being outdoors, as well as being creative. But she didn't uncover her touchstone until later in life as a result of having been transplanted to a new area.

C. L. majored in art at the University of Wisconsin, where she took weaving classes, then moved to San Diego and began working as a production weaver. After she'd designed wall hangings and clothing for seven years, her work evolved into painting images onto fiber to create patterned cloth. In the early 1980s, she decided that she wanted to change her main medium to paper and began to design collages for greeting cards. Motivated by a desire to earn more money, she altered her work, making collages with photos. By 1990, however, she began to feel the desire to expand her work and career progression but didn't have a clear sense of how to do that.

During a trip to San Francisco with her husband, C. L. decided that this was the perfect time to figure out what to do. She went for a drive and ended up at the zoo. As she watched the animals in their cages, she realized that there was a part of herself that had been held captive, too. Not fully comprehending how this revelation applied to her career, she sought professional advice. Her counselor helped C. L. recognize that she'd put part of herself in a prison, and that even her hand positions during these therapy sessions—closed fists—signified that she wasn't in a receiving mode. At this point, she realized that she needed to keep her eyes open for new opportunities.

Her husband was offered a position at Woods Hole on Cape Cod, so they moved there. Because she loved planting, tending, and even just looking at plants, and also because it was a way to spend time exploring her new environment, C. L. began to tour gardens on Cape Cod and photograph them. A new friend who worked as a publisher asked her if she could write horticultural advice to accompany her pictures, which he'd then publish.

In her wildest dreams, C.L. had never considered a career as a writer and garden expert. But here was the kind of new opportunity that she was looking for, and she seized it. She looked at her Values Orbit and decided to move gardening as a career into the inner orbit that art had once occupied. She combined her background and training in art, her newly rediscovered passion for the outdoors—a lifelong pursuit—and her self-training in all things garden-related, to launch an entirely new career for herself.

C. L. wrote her first book, *The Cape Cod Garden,* and soon a whole new world opened up before her. In addition to writing, C.L. started to speak about her new subject both locally and nationally, including at forums such as the Philadelphia Garden Show. Her appeal to audiences went beyond the borders of the flower beds: Her talks used gardening as a metaphor for life, career planning, and parenting. She emphasized growth, the concept of landscapes and life as works in progress, and the surprising "blossoms" that people can find along the way in both their gardens and their lives. By reconnecting with her love of the outdoors, C. L. realigned her Values Orbit to coincide with the life she wanted to lead.

She has now hit her stride and is doing the things she loves most. She continues to speak and write on gardening and has a weekly radio show and Website. One of her books, *Your Garden Shouldn't Make You Crazy!,* is sold nationwide in plant stores and nurseries. While she still has a general sense of how she wants her career to go, she's keeping herself open to new possibilities. She noted, "I love the element of surprise in gardening—you never know exactly how it's going to come out. And the same is true in life: I transplanted myself from California to Massachusetts, and blossomed where I was planted."

Personal Gardening Tips:

- Dig deep to reveal your "hidden blossom"—your touchstone—to put your Values Orbit in sync with the life you want to lead.

- Be proactive and jump-start your own life landscape plan. Only you can change your Values Orbit and begin the repotting process.

- Keep space in your life's garden to plant the new values you discover while doing these exercises. Transformation can't occur unless you first realign your Values Orbit to reflect your deepest value or touchstone.

You've seen how these three successful repotters shared an ability to courageously face the fact that past choices didn't allow them to fulfill their innermost needs. To bring their passions to the forefront of their lives, they needed to revamp their Values Orbit. The realization that significant change would be required to accomplish this realignment occurred at different times in the lives of each of these repotters. The "Aha!" moment can happen at any point. If you're ready to discover what's meaningful and begin to seek it, start drawing your Values Orbit—current and future—*now*.

You're ready to go to the next phase in your repotting process. To reach your goal, you'll need to research how and where to plant your seeds. Chapter 7 will help you think through the course of action necessary to pursue your chosen passion or interest based on your new Values Orbit.

Chapter Seven

Repotting Research:
Digging into Your Garden

Gardeners don't start on a final landscape design until they've completed a preliminary survey and base plan for their garden. This enables them to know the conditions—the available moisture and light, the soil type, and the climate zone. When they're ready to finalize their ideas, they evaluate all their research, as well as the various plants that are available and that they want to include. Shrubs, grass, trees, perennials, bulbs, and annuals are among the many elements to consider. For instance, most people probably wouldn't want a garden that contains only yellow plants on one side or that consists of only annuals and no perennials.

A gardener needs a well-defined strategy for developing a plan—what to plant when and where. In addition, she needs to decide what she can do herself and what tasks need to be outsourced, such as installing a watering system, planting trees, or creating structures, pathways, or screening. This isn't necessarily a solo activity—there's a wide variety of experts and advisers in every community who can assist her.

Just as gardeners devise a landscape strategy based on tangible factors, you, too, need to create a repotting strategy that incorporates all the elements of your base plan. By this time, after working through the exercises in the earlier chapters, you've completed your survey and your base plan, including putting more space, light, and fertilizer in your life and assessing the risks associated with change. It should be clear by now that you can't formulate an effective strategy overnight—it takes careful planning and accurate projections for the future. The linchpin is the thought process you undertake, which requires time and focus.

Think Week: A Bill Gates Approach to Pondering the Future

Microsoft chairman Bill Gates, one of the world's busiest and most successful business leaders, ponders the future of his company in a ritual of self-imposed seclusion that he calls "Think Week." Since the 1980s, he's set aside a week each year to contemplate the future of technology and the role that the Microsoft empire will play in it. He separates himself physically and mentally from his day-to-day life and responsibilities, only interrupting his thinking and researching time for meals.

Gates reads materials submitted by colleagues and staff and reviews a wide variety of media. He takes time to stroll on the waterfront in order to open his mind to new ideas. He knows that he can't access his own creativity or respond to the ideas of others unless he makes a radical change in his environment—it's too easy to be overwhelmed by the crush of daily life. Think Week provides him with the time and opportunity to become proactive rather than reactive, and it involves a three-step process: He has to make time to learn about new things, process the information, and respond by coming up with workable ideas.

Think Week for Repotters

Not everyone has a cabin on a lake, much less seven days to devote to their own version of Think Week. But to repot successfully, you must set aside a significant block of uninterrupted time to think through how you're going to pursue your passion and redesign your life. Without this mental and physical separation from your normal routine, you can't gain perspective or respond creatively to existing information and new ideas.

Like Bill Gates, you'll need to have access to your Idea File. As we mentioned earlier, this is a collection of the notes you made from previous exercises in this book. It should also contain any information you've gathered from networking and researching your passion, including ideas from the Internet, family, friends, and any articles you've collected along the way. Identify the important or big ideas you want to use in your repotting plan and write them on the appropriate page in the *Repotting 101* workbook or on a piece of paper that you entitle "Key Repotting Ideas." In addition, you'll need to identify any subject areas for further exploration. (We'll discuss ways to conduct additional research in the Repotting Research Clinic exercise that appears later in this chapter.)

Once you've gathered everything in your Idea File, you're ready to launch your own Think Week. In designing your personal retreat, remember that you can't change your life if you're conducting business as usual. To get the most out of this particular process, we recommend the following three steps:

1. Set time aside and create a think space. While you may not be able to allocate a full week for your own

Think Week, you must set aside a minimum of two hours a day for at least one week. Anything less than this won't allow you to think creatively, use your imagination, previsualize your redesigned life, and fully explore your passion and repotting goals. You also need to be physically separated from distractions such as family, pets, phone, TV, e-mail, and the like—no exceptions! If you can't find an appropriate space in your home, go elsewhere. You could use a friend's spare room, the library, or another quiet place.

2. Take time to read, learn, reflect, and organize your thoughts. Reread your notes and any materials you've already gathered in your Idea File. Identify any areas that need more research. Perhaps the Values Orbit exercise alerted you to a new interest or passion that you may want to explore. Also, new developments in your family or work situation might have cropped up, changing your environment and raising new questions. Organize your Idea File around such subjects as lifestyle, family, career, finances, learning, and health, so that you can see how each aspect of your life relates to the others as you assess your goal. The final part of this process is to develop an outline that shows you in black and white the key elements that will affect your repotting strategy. This step will help you focus on your motivators.

3. Brainstorm beyond the obvious. On your way to creating a strategy for a new life landscape, you must also take time to brainstorm about the possible results of your plan, as well as the unexpected consequences that may arise. For Exercises A and B that follow, use your *Repotting 101 Workbook* or your own materials to write down all the scenarios that you can imagine so that you can make informed and realistic decisions about your future.

Exercise A: "If . . . Then" Scenarios

It's not enough to identify the end result—the repotting goal—that you want to reach. It's essential to analyze the implications and effects of a major shift in your life. You'll need to think through the "If . . . then" scenarios of your proposed change. For instance, if you're thinking of becoming an entrepreneur, you can't simply educate yourself about the business aspects of this move. You must also think through questions that might arise, such as: *If I set up my own business and I'm the only employee, what happens if I or a member of my family becomes ill? Should I be thinking of a partnership arrangement rather than going solo? And beyond that, how would working with someone else affect my income, lifestyle, working environment, and so on?*

Thinking through all of the possible "If . . . then" scenarios will require a thorough examination. Your brainstorming process may involve consulting others for additional ideas or feedback. Make no mistake: This step is both essential and time-consuming—there are no shortcuts.

Exercise B: "What if . . ." Scenarios

Well-known consulting firms are now encouraging their corporate clients to think through and plan for unexpected outcomes as a key part of the development of a strategic plan. The effect of the events of 9/11 and Hurricane Katrina has been to make us all aware of outside forces that can dramatically change our lives at a moment's notice. While you can't anticipate everything that will impact you in the future, in order to repot successfully, you do need to consider unexpected scenarios—the good, the bad, and the ugly—that could conceivably impact your plan.

For example, let's say that you're a stay-at-home mom who has decided to go back to work. You've researched and prepared for all the logistical, financial, and lifestyle issues associated with this change. As part of your planning process, however, you need to look at "What if . . ." scenarios that you may never have considered. What would happen if your boss, who has promised you no travel as a part of your employment contract, is transferred, and your new supervisor wants you to take on clients in the field? You need to carefully weigh what you would do in this unplanned situation. If you knew ahead of time that this might happen, would you even contemplate taking this particular job?

As you go through your "What if . . ." checklist, be sure to think beyond the practical aspects of your plan and consider your emotional needs as well. In your excitement about embarking on a new life, don't overlook the fact that *you* may change in the process. What if you don't like your new pursuit? As we saw in Alice's story, her passion for cooking cooled when it became a 14-hour-a-day job. Consider what your emotions will be if you do make the leap, and if you don't.

At this point, some of you may have had a wake-up call. In spite of all your careful research and goal setting, you may have discovered that some of the "If . . . then" and "What if . . ." possibilities are too daunting at this time in your life. Even if you feel it's very unlikely that some of the worst-case scenarios will occur, you may not be able to face even a small risk that would negatively affect your current circumstances.

Take heart: There are other ways to redesign your life. Through the Repotting Research Clinic exercise, you may find the answers to some of your concerns. And for those of you who decide that a wholesale change in your life is currently not appropriate, the next chapter will illustrate how partial repotting is a viable alternative.

You may have to do further research to answer some of the questions that arise during your scenario-planning process. You may also need more information on how to pursue your goal, overcome potential obstacles, or zero in on your own feelings about your personal tolerance for risk and change. Our next exercise is designed to help you fill in the gaps on your way to developing a life landscape strategy.

Exercise: Repotting Research Clinic

When the time comes to decide which plants you're going to purchase to put in your garden, you may realize that you don't have enough information to proceed. You may have questions about what species would work best in your soil, where to buy the seeds or find exotic or unusual plants, and the compatibility of specimens that you plan to put together. Before you can finalize your landscape design, you may need to do some additional research.

Where do you start? Garden research uses the same sources that you'd use for your life landscape plan. These include the Internet, electronic and print media, community-based resources, and your own network and contacts. As you organized your Idea File, you probably came across questions that needed further inquiry. Now is the time to zero in on them and get appropriate information. Don't worry: If you don't know where or how to begin, this Repotting Research Clinic is designed to show you how to organize your investigation.

We know that each of you has your own set of motivations, circumstances, and repotting goals, as well as your own questions surrounding the process. While we don't know each of your individual questions, we can help you formulate an approach to find the answers. Your *Repotting 101 Workbook* includes pages for your research notes, or you can use your own materials.

In our interviews, many repotters told us that they had to grapple with a wide variety of questions to further explore the redesign of their life. They recognized that there was a gap between their vision and the practical steps they needed to take in order to make their vision a reality. To them, making a successful change was dependent upon being fully informed about all aspects of their goals. Since a majority of our interviewees wanted to repot by finding or starting a new career or by giving back as a path to fulfillment, our discussion below focuses on those areas. However, you can apply these same basic steps to whatever questions you're facing. But remember, not all the information or advice you receive will be valid for your own journey, so be careful to cull through everything to determine what applies to you!

Many potential repotters have uncovered a talent or passion that they want to pursue, but they need help translating that vision into reality. The first step is to understand the specific qualifications, requirements, or parameters of this pursuit, and that's what this exercise will help you do. There are several ways to find out what you'll need to do to transplant yourself: researching on the Internet and in the media, making the most of community-based resources, and tapping into your network—and beyond.

— **Researching on the Internet.** Do this at home, at work, or at your local library. The Internet is today's most efficient and limitless source of information about everything. Because this is such a vast resource, you'll need to focus your search with a well-crafted inquiry that will save you time and effort.

Let's say that you want to repot by changing careers. Many factors affected our interviewees' motivation to leave one job behind in favor of another. For some, the work they were doing wasn't satisfying or meaningful. For others, their position demanded too much time, effort, travel, or other sacrifice. In some cases, the urge stemmed from financial considerations or the feeling that their work didn't tap into their true passion.

The reasons you want to repot may range from your desire to find more personally rewarding work to wanting to join a more dynamic career sector. The good news is that some of the fastest-growing jobs offer both an opportunity to help others and high earning potential. These fields include education, nursing, information technology, business, and criminal justice. For instance, you might have identified health care as an area that appeals to you. Your Internet research may reveal nursing and health-care management as two possible avenues for you to pursue. It may even uncover a new area such as forensic nursing, a hot career opportunity that was virtually unknown ten years ago.

Follow every link that you need to in order to get the complete story on each career path—what it entails and how it might impact your life. As you do your research, take time not only to review the job descriptions and qualifications, but also to read any articles about available positions or profiles of individuals who are in this field. If you find that you'll need additional credentials, use the Internet to investigate whether or not local institutions offer relevant programs, or whether these qualifications can be obtained through online courses. Don't overlook your life experience or professional accomplishments, such as knowing a foreign language, as part of your skills set when applying for a degree program.

Some repotters may want to research how to work from home. The number of employed Americans who did this part-time (for as little as one day a year) or full-time grew to 44.4 million in 2004, according to a survey conducted by ITAC, the Telework Advisory Group for World at Work. If you're attracted to the idea of a 30-second commute because you care for children or aging parents, or for other reasons, then using the Internet to research home-based jobs would be a good starting point. For instance, the Internet lists the top telework-friendly positions that you can explore on **www.work-at-home-king.com**. If you're interested in franchise opportunities, start with **www.franchising. org**, or **www.nationalfranchising.com**.

Maybe you feel a job would add more meaning to your life but you have little or no experience or marketable skills. Don't worry—you can still repot and join the workforce. Several Websites list jobs that require no experience, but that allow you to get a foot in the door to start a new career. Have you ever thought of being a traffic technician? Did you know that all you need is a high school diploma and the average pay is over $37,000 a year? Or maybe you'd prefer to be an interviewer for a market-research firm. You can earn over $25,000 a year to start, and no college degree is required. If you're one of the 44 percent of all students who are enrolled at two-year colleges (or you want to be), you can find an excellent paying job with an associate degree. In this category, the highest paying positions are computer specialist ($59,000), nuclear technician ($59,000), dental hygienist ($58,000), radiation therapist ($57,000), and nuclear-medicine technologist ($55,000).

All kinds of career-related information can be found on the Internet. The part of the Resources section devoted to this chapter lists some Websites you can use as starting points.

— **Researching media.** Whether or not your Internet research has answered all your questions, another good resource is your local bookstore or library. There are hundreds of publications dedicated to specific fields of work and interests. From starting a business to home franchises to finance, there's a magazine or book that covers the subject. Spend an hour or so browsing through the publications on the rack, or visit the specific section in the bookstore devoted to your area of interest. If you can't or don't want to purchase these materials, you can access them at your local library. Check local radio and television listings to find programs covering career subjects of interest to you, and make time to watch or listen to these programs.

   — **Making the most of community-based resources.** Local community colleges, private colleges, and universities offer a myriad of adult-education classes as well as degree programs. Make an appointment to speak with the director of any of these to discuss course offerings and program requirements. You can either audit or register to take one class before you embark on a degree program to determine whether the options are right for you.

   There are other opportunities for learning off campus, in places like the local YMCA, junior college, or women's business center (see the Resources section for a listing in your area). You might also take a field trip to an institution, business, or other organization related to your proposed career change to research everything you can. For example, if you're interested in animals, visit a local veterinarian's office, volunteer at the local chapter of the Humane Society, or spend some time at your local pet retailer for ideas and inspiration—you may even end up with a new business idea!

   — **Tap into your network—and beyond.** Another key step in your research process is to tap into your human network. This includes talking to family members; friends; business colleagues; members of your school, church, garden or book club, gym, or investment group; neighbors; and friends of friends—in other words, everyone you come in contact with in your daily life.

   You should even get in touch with, and possibly interview, people you don't know who are in your field of interest. E-mail is a perfect way to start a conversation with someone you haven't met—just introduce yourself and outline your questions. As we found out while writing this book, most people are happy to respond to an invitation to talk about what they do and how someone else could enter their field.

We recognize that you might have some reservations about contacting others and asking for help. As we've said before, repotting requires courage and the willingness to step outside of what you would consider your normal boundaries and comfort zone. Don't hesitate to think of your network in the broadest possible sense. The person sitting next to you on the bus may be a stepping-stone to your new career.

At this point, be sure that the information and notes generated by your research is gathered and organized in one place. (If you're using the *Repotting 101 Workbook,* it's already organized for you.)

Elizabeth's Story

Elizabeth had been in the government-relations department at a trade association for more than 15 years, dedicating long hours to the job. Her hard work earned her the respect of her peers, and she was elected president of a nonprofit association of women in government-relations positions. She also finally became a lobbyist for her trade association, an impressive achievement in the then-male-dominated energy field. Although she had several more years ahead of her before retirement, she'd begun to feel bored with her legislative work, was tired of the demanding hours, and was often tempted to shift her focus entirely.

She began to think seriously about life after lobbying, taking time in the evenings and on weekends to consider what changes she wanted to make in her life. Her Think Week lasted longer than seven days—she actually considered her goals and options over the course of several months—but the process was an important first step in providing her with the new information on which to build her repotting plan.

To begin with, she realized that she wanted more control over her schedule and was eager to spend more time with her family: her husband, her six stepchildren, and her aging mother. For Elizabeth, getting out from under a full-time position was crucial. In addition, she realized that she wasn't ready to stop working entirely. She enjoyed being productive and busy and had no interest in a post-career lifestyle of golf and bridge, even though she enjoyed both of these pastimes. So she decided to focus on finding a way to incorporate into her next life stage the thing she enjoyed most but had the least time to do in her current position—travel. Her challenge was figuring out how to combine this with some kind of paying work.

In her earlier years, Elizabeth had lived and traveled extensively in Africa and other countries. She was excited and energized by seeing new places and unfamiliar cultures, and longed to incorporate such new experiences into her post-career life. How to make travel a central part of her existence after a career in lobbying became her main focus. With her already well-developed problem-solving skills, she set out to address the question of finding a new identity for herself.

Elizabeth began her research by consulting with a close friend who shared her passion for travel and Africa. They spent many hours discussing what they loved most about seeing the world and considering how they could afford to do this in the way they wanted. They decided that their initial goal would be to use their expertise and knowledge of Africa to lead customized tours there for like-minded friends and family members—and to have fun together in the process. Their fees for organizing and leading the trips would pay for their own expenses and could provide start-up money for a new business. But since neither one of them had ever run a company before, further research was necessary.

Elizabeth's next step was to consult a number of travel agents she'd worked with during her professional life. After these conversations, she determined that she did *not* want to be a travel agent per se—in other words, she didn't want to learn how to write and issue plane tickets and become a member of ASTA, the travel agents' trade association. Instead, she and her friend decided that their niche would be to offer the benefit of their long experience in Africa and their willingness to customize trips for clients who wanted a unique and personalized experience. They'd use discounters and other experts in the ticket-writing field but not do that work themselves.

Elizabeth kept working full time and continued her research process by exploring the current marketplace. She began to collect brochures from existing travel companies and to look into similar offerings on the Internet. She came away from this research and her ongoing discussions with her friend with a clear understanding of how they should position their company.

She also continued to network with travel agents, taking them to lunch to "pick their brains" on all aspects of running a customized tour business. In one casual conversation, someone happened to refer to trip insurance. Elizabeth was momentarily stunned—this was something she and her partner hadn't even considered! After her contact explained the liability issues to her, she realized that this major expense would have to be factored into her business plan.

Now that the two friends were equipped with the results of their extensive field research, they still needed to establish a plan for getting clients. They'd already spoken with individuals who'd said that they'd be interested in joining an African tour. But Elizabeth realized that she might need a plan for promoting the business beyond people she knew and called on a contact from her network who ran a marketing company.

Although this person's professional advice was logical and practical, in the long run Elizabeth and her partner found that referrals would form the basis for their clientele. They did try to advertise, but found out the hard way that the personal aspect that distinguished their company from other tour operators wasn't easy to translate into print. Despite receiving many responses to the ads, they never got a client that way. In other words, they found, as you may, that not all of the advice they gathered in the research phase was valid.

Elizabeth finally took the biggest step toward repotting into her new life: She retired. Then she and her partner immediately began to plan their first trip for the friends and family who'd already committed to be the "guinea pigs" for their new business. The rest is history. In the past ten years, Elizabeth and her partner have gone beyond offering trips to Africa to leading groups to Madagascar, Budapest, Australia, New Zealand, and many other destinations. Although they did extensive research before repotting, they've continued to learn on the job as well.

Elizabeth says that having a partner was a key part of her successful repotting. She has enjoyed sharing the ups and downs of running the business with a close friend, and credits the association as the source of the venture's success. But she does advise anyone who's thinking of changing her life in a significant way to spend the time to research her idea. She noted, "Although your research probably can't cover everything you need to know, you can avoid a lot of mistakes and pitfalls by doing your homework ahead of time."

Sigrid's Story

Sigrid was born and raised in Iceland, but at the age of 19, she took a vacation in the U.S. and met her future husband during the first week of the trip. She married and moved to the United States, where she finished her B.A. and then worked as a tour guide for the Foreign Service Institute. She raised four sons and was active in school and church affairs.

One of her sons spent a year abroad living in Germany. The following year, Sigrid agreed to host a German foreign-exchange student in her home. This was the seed that led her to begin researching how she could repot from her life as an active stay-at-home mother to a professional counselor.

The student was a very difficult and arrogant teenager who created many challenging situations for Sigrid and her family during the course of his stay. To try to deal with the young man's behavioral problems, she took time off from her other activities to reflect on ways to help him. She worked with him on a regular basis, trying to help him make the transition from being a moody adolescent who didn't know how to set personal limits to being a mature young man. Although she hadn't expected to have to counsel this visitor in such an in-depth way, Sigrid realized at the end of the year that she'd not only helped him, but had also discovered a talent she didn't know she possessed.

She began to reflect about a possible career for herself in counseling teenagers and parents. Her Think Week was actually more like a "Think Year," as she used the time with the exchange student to identify her skills and think about using them outside the home once her children had graduated from high school.

Sigrid realized that one of her primary values was helping other people. She'd seen a therapist herself for some personal problems and realized how her interest in helping others could be translated into a profession. Once she decided that she wanted to turn her counseling skills into a career, she began to research the steps she'd need to take to make her choice a reality.

First, she talked to her family. Her husband and children were very supportive of her idea to go back to school for training. Her friends were also positive, and some told her that they wished they had the courage to break out of their current lives to try something new, too. Sigrid then met with faculty members at several local universities about degree programs. She identified community counseling as her chosen field, took the graduate school entrance exam, and was admitted as a student in 2003. For the next two years, she attended classes and worked at local hospitals and family centers as a counselor to acquire field experience.

Her thorough research and planning has paid off. Now Sigrid has graduated with a degree in community counseling and is working to accumulate enough hours in fieldwork to obtain her official license. She's finding that her new professional life is energizing and interesting.

Sigrid told us that her advice to other women would be to find what they enjoy and what energizes them, and also identify what they do well. This takes time and careful thought, and the answer isn't always immediately clear. Once they've found the key to unlocking their potential, though, they'll be "ready to roll," according to Sigrid.

Transplanting Yourself Out of a Career

A number of repotters told us that after their brainstorming sessions, they realized that what they really wanted to do was find fulfillment by giving back to the world and their communities. Their professional and monetary accomplishments, while rewarding, weren't meeting their personal need to help others outside of their immediate families. Some of our interviewees came to this realization after spending many years building successful careers or companies. Others may or may not have been working but told us that something was missing in their lives.

There was no one path to follow for all of these women—each had to find her own way—although they shared a common ambition to channel their desire to make a contribution to society. But how do you find a way to give back that fits with your time requirements, areas of interest, and overall repotting goal? This requires both research and careful planning on your part. It may even involve trial and error.

Here are some steps you can follow that are based upon suggestions from our interviewees about their own experiences. Make notes as you go through Steps 1 through 5, either in your *Repotting 101 Workbook* or using your own materials.

Step 1: Tap into your Values Orbit to find what interests you. Between creating your Values Orbit and doing the Think Week exercises, you may have found that you not only want to volunteer, but also that you know which missions inspire you. You might have an interest that's related to something you're somewhat involved with now or that was a part of your life in the past. Check your Idea File and make a list of what inspires you to want to volunteer your time, talents, and skills.

Once you've identified your cause, use the suggestions given earlier in this chapter and research what nonprofit organizations related to your interest exist in your community. Part of this process is determining whether you want to volunteer in an area you already know or branch out into something entirely new. Sticking with what you know may help smooth the transition from what you're currently doing to volunteering, but changing the focus of your philanthropic work may offer the challenge and stimulation you're seeking.

Step 2: Recognize that starting something new may mean starting small. When contacting nonprofits to inquire about a possible volunteer position, remember that your career or life experience may not translate immediately into a leadership position. Indeed, you may even start part-time to see if the group is right for you. Some of our interviewees joined several different organizations simultaneously to experiment with which mission was the best to fulfill their overall values.

Step 3: Know what you want. In a *Wall Street Journal* article on retirement, author Kelly Greene noted that " . . . you want to do something meaningful as a volunteer, and that's reward enough." But other considerations may be just as valid. You might get satisfaction from the relationships you develop and the sense of purpose you feel when you're involved in a cause that helps others. These factors could be just as important to you as the ideal you originally embraced, such as helping children or funding cancer research.

Step 4: Know your boundaries and yourself. How will you fit volunteering into your life? You need to determine what proportion of your Time Savings Bank is going to be devoted to volunteering, and weigh that against your need for personal freedom. If you make the choice to leave a career in order to give back to the community, be careful that your volunteer efforts don't consume so much of your life that you face the same problem that you did in your paid work: not enough time for family or other personal priorities. Finding the correct balance may take a period of trial and error. Keeping your options open regarding how you fill your free moments—the fallow beds you created in your revised Personal Garden Calendar —doesn't mean that you have to waste them. Clearly communicate your time commitment to people in the organization you've chosen so that they understand your limits.

As you'll see in the next chapter, experimentation is a useful first step in Repotting 101. Trial and error may also be part of finding the right volunteer work for you. Sometimes, the tasks you signed up for don't fit your skills, or the position just isn't what you expected. You may not like attending meetings at night, or more important, the mission or goals of the organization may not mesh exactly with your own. Recognize that your first, second, and even third volunteering efforts may not work out. Be flexible, keep trying, and eventually you'll bring together the elements you care about the most.

Step 5: Start your own volunteer organization. If you can't find an activity that meets your needs on all levels, you may feel the urge to start your own nonprofit. Realize that this kind of bootstrap operation takes dedication and determination, but it may be the most satisfying mission for you. Family or life circumstances (such as a child's illness) may lead you to create an organization that responds to those situations. Several of our interviewees repotted into mission-oriented lives because they were driven to help their own children. If you're considering starting your own venture, you should consult others in your area of interest to learn the pros and cons of doing so.

Teresa's Story

Teresa majored in journalism, took paralegal courses, and dreamed of being a lawyer one day. However, she also knew from a very early age that she loved children. After following her spouse to various cities while he pursued a law degree, she finally settled down with him to start a family. Soon afterward, she realized that she needed to have more contact with other moms and wanted a place for her children to socialize.

She started a mother/child playgroup that kept growing until she had to find space in a local church and started charging for membership. Teresa's three children attended the group, which she ran without pay as a volunteer. At the time, she said, "My children were happy making friends, and I was meeting other moms and feeling like I was doing something worthwhile." When her fourth child was born with a hearing disability, she knew that she'd have to stop this volunteer work and focus on him. She sold what had now become a preschool and paid herself back for all the years of work she'd invested.

Teresa needed to find a way to help her son. Her research led her to a then-new procedure called a "cochlear implant," which was being performed at Johns Hopkins Hospital. After she did more research and discussed it with her husband and the doctors, her son successfully underwent the operation. But there was a problem: There was no rehabilitation program for children who had received cochlear implants.

Teresa knew that she had to do something about this. Moving once again from being a stay-at-home mom caring for her son into taking on a volunteer position, she became the coordinator of the largest implant-rehabilitation program in the U.S., located at Johns Hopkins. By helping her son, she was also assisting others. As she told us, "If you care about something, get involved and get experience—even the volunteer positions women have can lead to something more." Teresa was becoming a social entrepreneur—led there by her son, her interest in helping other children, and a desire to make the world a better place.

During her tenure at the hospital, Teresa decided that she needed more credentials in order to have a career working with hearing-impaired children and obtained a master's degree in developmental psychology and language development. Having worked with many doctors who were professors, she got recommendations, took the Graduate Record Examinations (GRE), and applied only to the Johns Hopkins program. Over the course of two years, her days included driving children to school; going to the hospital to volunteer; returning home for car-pool pickup, dinner, and homework; and then going back out to take classes at night.

While looking for schools for her son, Teresa had an epiphany—that children like him should be allowed to learn in mainstream school settings. She knew that she didn't want to treat this child differently from the rest of her family, and she wanted other deaf children to have an opportunity to have a mainstream school experience. So with the help of some M.B.A. candidates who'd worked with her on the business plan for the rehab program, she started to develop a plan for a school that would be a model for how deaf children can learn in regular classrooms.

By the time Teresa graduated from her master's program, she'd already made a business plan, incorporated the new school, raised start-up money, hired an initial team, and bought a building. She was well on the way to launching a learning institution that incorporated hearing, nonhearing, and cochlear-implant students.

Today, the school, which opened in 2000, is a model for national and international hearing-disabled teaching professionals.

> **Personal Gardening Tip:** To successfully transplant yourself, dream large, dig and delve, and weed selectively. Gather all your resources and learn and research everything about your new ideas—your seeds and plants—before you begin the repotting process. Visualize the right plant in the right place at the right time.

What you've collected in your *Repotting 101 Workbook* or your own Idea File will help you start creating your new life landscape plan. Next, you have to organize your information and make time to think about it. Once you've identified what areas to weed out and what data is missing, conduct research to find the answers you need. Then you'll be ready to take your repotting plan and plant your redesigned life landscape.

You may learn that you're unwilling or not ready to make a wholesale change. If that's the case, partial repotting may be the answer for you. The next chapter shows how some women tackle the process of change one step at a time.

Partial Repotting:
Cultivating One Flower Bed at a Time

Once she's completed her final landscape plan, a gardener should be ready to proceed with her project. But before she buys and installs plants, she may want to pause and evaluate whether or not she can undertake a wholesale uprooting and replanting of her garden at this time. There may be a series of reasons why she decides to do a partial change rather than a full-scale redesign.

The Time Challenge

A key concern may be the time required to repot. A gardener needs to ask herself how much time she has available and whether it's enough to allow her to undertake this major project. In addition, she must consider the conditions and timing (that is, whether it's the right season). In previous chapters, we've looked extensively at the time issue in women's lives. Your decision to plunge into a full-scale repotting process or to take it one step at a time is directly linked to how much time you can devote to recalibrating your life. Even though you've now defined your passion and the direction you want to go, only you can decide whether it's the right point to embark on a major overhaul or not.

Many of our interviewees told us that even though they were satisfied with their new goals and proposed changes and felt comfortable with their plans, they simply weren't ready to go forward full-steam ahead. Instead, many of them decided to test the waters by taking a phased approach to the repotting process.

Financial Concerns

Time may be only one of several issues facing a gardener as she prepares to plant. The financial cost of a major overhaul may determine whether or not she can launch a full or partial garden-redesign plan. She might decide that planting in stages fits her budget better than a full-scale landscaping project does; she may want to upgrade one flower bed at a time.

For repotters, a phased approach can provide a trial period to see if the financial aspects of their strategy will work. There are a variety of issues that can encourage partial repotting. The plan may involve a pay cut, an interruption of the current income stream, new expenses in the form of start-up costs or tuition, or factors that may impact the family budget in other ways. For example, a woman undergoing repotting may choose to go from a full-time job to a part-time one, instead of leaving her work altogether. This partial move may become a permanent one, depending on her finances. For some, a total change isn't possible or even desirable.

Life Interruptions

Almost as important as time and money issues for a gardener is the question of disruption to her life and environment. Does she really want to tear up her entire backyard just as summer is coming and her family would most like to enjoy the lawn? Also, supervising the various aspects of the project—from deliveries to consultations with landscape architects to the installation of a sprinkler system—may be disruptive to the gardener and her family's schedule.

Whether you're single or married, repotting can cause major disruptions. The changes you make can affect everything from your schedule to the allocation of responsibilities in your family to your overall lifestyle. For some women, partial repotting is the only answer because the parameters of their life are fixed. Some repotters are constrained in their choices by their children's school schedules. This can be true whether women are single or married with a husband whose career makes it impossible for him to help out with domestic duties in a significant way. Partial repotting allows women to go through the necessary period of upheaval that accompanies any change to see if they can handle it and what the ripple effects will be.

A Partial Solution

A gardener may determine that the original project is beyond what she can take on at this time. The best-laid plan can't always be implemented because circumstances change. Or, in the final evaluation, a gardener may have determined that, in fact, only one flower bed or section of the yard *needs* to be redone. And finally, it may be that someone starts small because she simply wants to see how the project goes before she expands it.

In the same way, the pace of repotting will vary according to each woman's individual goals, personality, and lifestyle issues. Some may want to start slowly, while others might move at a faster pace. In this chapter, we'll focus on women selected took this "fractional formula"—that is, those who chose to make a partial life landscape change. Their reasons for this decision may vary—from wanting to experiment before committing to a particular plan, to acknowledging that only a partial repotting is feasible for financial or other reasons, to realizing that they just want to start small.

In addition, many repotters are part of a growing trend among retirees called "flex-retirement." In a *Wall Street Journal* article, this term was defined as "reduced, but continuing, work—combined with a cultivation of leisure activities—sometimes beginning well before age 65 and extending long past it." For these women, flex-retirement offers an alternative to the nine-to-five grind and a way to pursue other interests. Partial repotting offers older working women the intangible benefits of work—the opportunity to learn something new, to feel valued, and to socialize with others—as well as the freedom to pursue their passions and the chance to gain financial security.

You may choose this route because it will offer you the opportunity to gain information, feedback, and confirmation about the plan you've developed and the choices you've made. Your pilot program is your chance to experiment—with the passion or goal you selected, the impact on your life, and the practical logistics of making it happen.

Let's say that your repotting objective is to get an advanced degree to help you launch a career, change fields, or enhance your marketability. You start with night school in order to try out your plan and everything it entails, from tuition and the cost of books to the stamina required for such an extended day and the impact on your life. After attending classes, you determine that going back to school right now is too much for you and that an online degree program tailored to your own schedule is an even better idea.

Partial repotting offers the chance to plant a seed to see if it will grow, without having to commit to an entire garden. This is your opportunity to take your idea for a reengineered life for a test drive. There are several possible outcomes.

First, you may confirm that you're on the right track and are ready to fully repot. A mother of three children who experimented with making dog collars and leashes on a small scale in her community found this home-based venture totally satisfying. The business took off, so she began to market the products nationally. She continued to run things from home, allowing her to tend to her family.

Second, you may discover that partial repotting is as far as you want to go to incorporate a new component in your life. A highly successful businesswoman in the events-planning field scaled back her work life in order to pursue decorative painting. She found that although she loved this artistic outlet, for her, it couldn't replace the stimulation of running her company. She returned to the corporate world full-time, but preserved the time for pursuing her art on weekends and during vacations.

Third, you may learn that you love the overall structure of your redesigned life, but you need to rework the details. Another mother of three decided to dedicate herself to philanthropic causes. She determined that what she really wanted to do was to start her own foundation to pursue the mission and goals that she feels are important.

And finally, your partial-repotting experience may reveal that the area you've chosen to pursue isn't the best fit for you or it isn't the right time for you to make a change. In this case, you may decide to put your plans on the shelf for now and revisit them in the future, or you may try to identify another repotting goal. We told you in an earlier chapter about a young woman who repotted from clinical psychology to become a professional pastry chef. She realized that in practice, the culinary world wasn't for her. She went back to square one and became the owner of successful pet-care company.

As you learned earlier in this book, there can be unexpected or unintended surprises in your garden, as well as in your repotting process. Partial repotters may find that the process of taking a new path is a valuable experience in itself. One woman (described more fully in "Karen's Story," page 153) told us that her partial repotting process—moonlighting as a masseuse—was such an expansive growth experience that it inspired her to return to her original full-time career and find new ways to make it more fulfilling. With a fresh mind-set, she was able to express her nurturing side in her original workplace.

We believe that partial repotting can be an integral step in the overall process. It serves as a pilot project that allows women to evaluate the choices they've made without causing major disruption to their lives or finances.

They may decide to remain partial repotters because that solution offers them the best of both worlds: the opportunity to change without having to completely overhaul their lives.

No matter what stage you're in or what age you are, if you do decide to repot, starting small is a great way to begin. The stories below illustrate how partial repotting may facilitate a redesign of your life landscape plan.

Karen's Story

Karen graduated from the University of Virginia with a B.A. in religious studies. After graduation, she married and became a real estate broker. Discovering that she hated sales, she was then drawn to the analysis involved in real estate appraisal and started to work in this field. Because she loved it so much, she decided to start her own company as a way to gain greater financial rewards and a more flexible schedule for raising her children.

To get her business going, Karen followed all the necessary research steps, including consulting her network, gathering information on the market in her community, and determining the licensing and other requirements for owners of a real-estate-appraisal business. When she felt her plan was complete, with the necessary loans and staff in place, she launched her company with a focus on residential sales. Later, after taking various courses and certification programs, she expanded into commercial real estate appraisal.

In addition to building her career and raising a family, Karen also found a way to incorporate personal interests into her life. She mentored young girls in a reading program and joined a local rowing team. She often became sore from her workouts and used regular massage as therapy. Responding to the healing aspects of massage, and her need to find something more fulfilling than her current work, she decided to investigate massage therapy as a possible new career.

As she started to consider repotting yet again, Karen interviewed other therapists and gathered relevant information. She enrolled in a masseuse certificate program, taking courses at night while running her business in the day, and graduated after 18 months. At this point, her repotting goal was to form a group practice with other masseuses she knew and sell her real estate appraisal business.

Karen's experiment began with her offering massage therapy to clients two evenings a week while continuing to run her business. She discovered that while she liked the nurturing and healing aspects of massage, along with the contact with her clients, she loved her real estate appraisal work even more, including the financial rewards it offered.

More important, Karen found that this partial repotting proved to be very expansive, allowing her to discover that she had, as she said, "the power to make changes that would allow my role in my business to suit me even more." She decided that she'd continue to work in real estate appraisal and just change her mind-set and management approach to suit her own needs.

Karen is now living the life of a partial repotter. When she determined that a key priority in her Values Orbit was to bring more harmony and spirituality into her life through helping others, she initiated the repotting process, adding the new component of massage to her life, as well as a fresh approach to her business. Along the way, however, she learned that she was unwilling to turn away from the company she'd worked so hard to start and grow.

Her life today represents the merging of two important values: the independence and challenge of being an entrepreneur in a field she loves and her desire for a more nurturing connection with her clients. Today, she's fulfilled by managing her successful company and giving massages to clients twice a week. When she retires from her appraisal business, Karen expects to continue to do massage on a part-time basis.

Your repotting process may result in a partial solution in which you replant only one bed. Your own reasons for this choice may differ from Karen's, but they're still valid. There's no one final answer for all repotters. Your own personal landscape plan may end short of a total redesign of your life. If that's what works for you—as it did for Karen—then engaging in the process of partial repotting may be worth the effort.

Sarah's Story

Sarah is a young, single, working woman living in a major American city. As an undergraduate at a prominent business school, she majored in finance and thought she'd work in that field. From an early age, her dream was to be an entrepreneur. Even as a five-year-old visiting Times Square, she told her parents, "This would be a great place to put a lemonade stand."

After graduation, Sarah took a job in market research with a leading beauty company, and later worked for a competitor in the same field. Her marketing and research skills were well known, and subsequently, she was recruited by a major gourmet-food manufacturer. Throughout the first five years she worked after graduation, her head was filled with new business ideas, and she never lost sight of her goal to start her own business. As she told us, "Going out on my own had been a passion for a long time. I was just waiting for the right idea."

One day, she came back to the office after lunch with a blister on her foot, and no one in her office had a Band-Aid. A few days later, she spilled soup on her skirt; nobody had any stain remover. She came up with the idea for a catchall kit with products that you can never find when you need them. After talking to friends and colleagues about her concept, she decided to moonlight as an entrepreneur and start a kit business from her home.

Keeping her day job to pay the bills, Sarah launched her company but relied on her family to fill any orders as they came in. She created a Website and has met with several major retailers in the hope of getting a large order that will put her on the map. Her ultimate repotting goal is to do this full-time, but for now, she's in the experimental stage.

Sarah is a partial repotter hoping to become a full-scale one. She has every intention of leaving her current job and managing and growing her kit business from home on a full-time basis—and her vision doesn't end there. She sees herself starting other entrepreneurial ventures after she sells this one. For her, visualizing success is a key component of the repotting process. Running her kit business on the side is merely part of a phased plan. She anticipates moving from partial to full-blown repotting in the near future.

Both Sarah's and Karen's stories illustrate the value of the partial approach to repotting. There's no substitute for experience along the road to making a major life decision. Experimenting with something new can provide you with stimulation and valuable insight into your current life and your plans for the future. In the initial phase, you may uncover unexpected nuggets of knowledge about yourself that will be useful whether or not you choose to go any further. Whether you partially repot to test your vision or because this is the level of change you want in your life, you're likely to grow and blossom along the way.

Exercise: Partial Repotting Readiness Evaluation

It's important to evaluate whether the experiment you may undertake is the right one, and whether you should proceed with a more extensive garden overhaul. The next exercise will help you do just that, and it may also encourage you to choose partial repotting as your final life landscape plan. Or you may decide to identify a new passion to pursue. You might even choose to resume your old life because the new plan doesn't work for you. Only you can make the final determination about what your next move will be.

The questions that follow are designed to help you make an accurate assessment of your repotting process. Please answer them *Yes* or *No* in your *Repotting 101 Workbook* or on a separate piece of paper.

1. Is how you've chosen to reinvent yourself—by pursuing a new interest, lifestyle, career, and so on—the right decision? (The good news is that no shift is irreversible or set in stone.)

2. If you're uneasy about the change you're contemplating is the problem the passion you've selected or your approach to pursuing it? (If your approach is the problem, don't be discouraged; there are many ways to plant a garden. It may take three or more tries for you to find the right plan for yourself.)

3. Have you provided enough time to test the idea—to let blossoms emerge? (Every change requires a different time investment. Remember, just as there are no instant gardens, there are no instant results. Take the time *you* need to come to terms with your new life.)

4. Has one of the challenges in your repotting process emerged as an obstacle that you're unable to overcome? (For instance, are the financial issues caused by your proposed change too difficult for you to handle, or is your family not able to cooperate with the variation in your availability? These and other reasons have caused some women to forgo a more extensive repotting or to start over.)

5. Is your partial repotting effort a workable, doable, and preferable way to go about changing your life? Or do you now feel energized

enough to proceed with a wholesale redesigned life landscape plan? If you've embarked upon this experiment thinking that partial repotting was just a first step but now feel that it's enough for you, don't worry. One of the unexpected outcomes of repotting may be the decision to transplant only one aspect of your life.

Personal Gardening Tip: Experimentation is a critical step in redesigning your life landscape plan. Test your hypothesis: Is your chosen passion or interest—the new plants in your flower bed—right for you?

Chapter Nine

Cultivating a New Life and Transplanting Successfully

A gardener's ultimate goal is to put more beauty into her life with a finished product that will be visually rewarding throughout the four seasons. She may also want settings where she can nurture her personal and spiritual growth. But she can't achieve those goals without careful attention to detail and a final review of her overall landscape master plan. Designing this blueprint requires extensive planning, field research, investigation of alternatives, and informed decision making. Once the plan is complete, she has to do a reality check and look it over to be sure that she's considered all facets of the site and the process.

No matter how large or small the scope of the overall project is, a gardener needs to understand how the various elements will work together. She must build a solid foundation to ensure that all the elements complement each other and work together to form a coherent whole. To achieve a workable design, she should balance the *hardscape*—a term landscape designers use to describe those unchangeable aspects of a garden, such as structures and environmental conditions—and the *softscape*—the term for the elements that can be changed, such as foliage, plants, shape, and design. Along the way to achieving the final layout, a gardener may find that she needs to steer her way through a thicket of alternatives and options. The ability to focus yet remain open to change is a critical part of carrying out a master landscape plan that works.

For a repotter, the ultimate goal is finding the right portal to achieving a more meaningful and fulfilling life. To do so, she must finalize her personal landscape plan, which depends on building a good foundation, putting the right pieces in the right places, balancing what can be changed with what can't, and doing a reality check to be sure it's all feasible.

In earlier chapters, you've been encouraged to analyze your life in terms of your time; your mental, physical, and spiritual condition; and your willingness to take risks. We hope you've been able to identify your key passion or interest and establish a new goal for self-fulfillment. In the process, you've determined what additional resources and skills you'll need to help you reach your goal. You may even have experimented with your newly reconfigured life and made adjustments according to what you learned about yourself in this trial period.

Now it's time to take a final hard look at your repotting plan. Ask yourself: *Have I created a solid foundation on which to build a new life landscape? Are all the pieces in place to launch the repotting process with the greatest chance of success? Do I have a clear understanding of how all the elements will work together?*

Finding Your Green Thumb

Congratulations! You've almost reached the finish line along the road to becoming a bona fide repotter. Gardeners know that to avoid trouble, it's easier to erase and redraw their plans at this stage than it is to dig and haul earth later. Landscape designers use the term "field adjustments" to describe their process of finding solutions and fixing problems before the final installation. Take your time dreaming and planning to ensure that what you have on paper is what you want in life.

Before launching your strategy, you need to do a final analysis to give you perspective. The next two exercises are designed to help you do just that. The first one will help you see how your life after repotting will look on paper—the foundation of your plan, the various pieces, and how they'll all work together. The ultimate purpose is to determine whether the change you're planning is workable for you. The second exercise is designed to help you focus on the timing of representative tasks involved in initiating and following through on your plan.

Exercise: Your Garden Reality Check—A Planting Prerequisite

This final, dispassionate review of your personal landscape plan is an important step toward making a successful transition into your new life. Doing this exercise will give you an opportunity to go through the checklist for your repotting tool kit and be sure you have all the right tools at hand. It will also provide a mental and emotional framework as you begin. What's more, thinking through all aspects of your plan will provide you with the reassurance and confidence that you're prepared for what you're contemplating and can deal with the unexpected.

To do this exercise, refer to your *Repotting 101 Workbook* or use your own materials.

Step 1: Get out the spiral notebook we encouraged you to buy at the beginning of this book, or use a plain piece of paper. Create two columns; label one "Hardscape" and the other "Softscape."

Step 2: In the "Hardscape" column, list all those things that you feel are difficult if not impossible to change. Include anything that circumscribes your life and your decision-making process—the factors that set boundaries and limits on your endeavors. These items might include your family situation, cultural factors, health issues, or financial circumstances.

As you're contemplating this list, be sure that the issues really are Hardscape ones, and that you haven't overlooked alternative approaches to dealing with them. For instance, you may feel that your family dynamics are a stumbling block to your taking courses or a new job because you do everything for your husband and children, and no one else contributes. Have you explored creative approaches to problem solving with your family members? Are there ways for them to take on some responsibilities, freeing you up to pursue your goals? This approach may ultimately benefit everyone.

Step 3: In the "Softscape" column, list all those factors that can be shifted or altered to suit your newly redesigned life. Include anything you've decided is optional, from tasks you can outsource to beauty treatments, entertainment, and satisfying other people's agendas.

Be sure that both lists are honest and realistic. Remember, you may not always achieve your final objective, but the journey toward your goal can provide its own rewards. In the process of doing this exercise, you may decide that pursuing some of the alternatives and options that you've identified and researched throughout Part II of this book is actually the right course and should supplant certain elements of your original plan. If so, now is the time to commit to those decisions and make the adjustments.

Step 4: Seek input on your entire plan from a friend, mentor, spouse, or relative. Select someone whom you respect, but more important, who will honor your expectations and provide you with valid feedback. You'll either incorporate suggestions from this person or not. Even though you've conferred with your network during the research phase, now you're engaging in the final planning stage of your repotting—determining the who, what, when, where, and why. In this final consultation, your friend, mentor, spouse, or relative will serve as a sounding board for you.

As in a garden, redesigning your life requires flexibility on all levels, combined with the ability to persevere and dedicate yourself to your repotting journey. Along the way, you'll have the opportunity to pick and choose what's right for you, keeping some elements and discarding others until you get the appropriate bouquet or combination for you. Your goal isn't to create the perfect life, but rather to bring the meaning and fulfillment you're seeking into a situation that actually works for you. Now it's time to put theory into practice—to create a repotting timeline.

Your Personal Garden Almanac

We all know that the best-laid plans can fail without proper execution. Gardeners understand that for their ventures to be successful, timing is everything—for instance, the seasons will dictate the planting schedule. Bulbs should be placed in the fall, annuals can't go in during the winter, and the best time to condition the soil is in the spring. Gardeners pace their tasks to be sure that plants are provided with the proper nutrient balance and other essential elements when they're most needed.

Just as knowing when to plant is key for gardeners, timing is essential for repotters. As the architect of your own life, you're now ready to create a timeline for executing your repotting plan. At this point, you need to tie your strategy to a realistic schedule with appropriate milestones and checkpoints along the way.

It's clear from our interviews that each repotter moves at a different pace. Your timeline will reflect your own set of circumstances and personality and lifestyle issues. To set your plan in motion, you must have a starting point and markers along the way to lead you toward your goal. This shouldn't be set in stone, however, since we all know that life can be unpredictable. Just as April snowstorms may delay your gardening plans, unexpected events may alter your timeline.

Sample checklists and timelines are included in the *Repotting 101 Workbook,* or you can refer to the Landscape

Master Plan, which begins on page 207. As you develop your repotting strategy according to this timeline exercise, you'll need to refer back to your Think Week materials from Chapter 7, especially the "What if . . ." scenarios. For every task or issue you address in your timeline, be sure you've thought through alternatives and created a backup plan (or "Plan B"), in case things don't work out or there are unexpected developments along the way.

You'll need a Plan B so that you can respond to any surprises that occur, whether positive or negative. For example, let's say you start a home-based business while still working part-time at your current job and plan to evaluate your progress at the end of six months. But things take off right away, and you need to make an immediate decision about quitting your current job and putting all your energy into the home venture. Or what if you start a new job and your child-care provider quits in the middle of the week, leaving you with young children at home and no backup support? What's your Plan B?

Repotting Philosophy

Your life, like a garden, is a work in progress. Nothing is static; everything is in flux. As we've found in our own lives and in talking with our numerous interviewees, an essential element for successful repotting is the discipline of making time to stop and reflect on where you've been, where you are now, and where you're going. According to a *Washington Post* article, "[In a garden,] impatience . . . and indifference are two reasons many landscape designs don't reach their greatness." Repotters don't exist in a vacuum. As you move forward with a plan, the multiple pieces of your life are changing as well. You'll need to periodically review and evaluate how all these shifting parts are working together.

Each repotter will approach this evaluation process differently. One told us that she had to review her progress in reaching her goals on a daily basis in order to stay focused on implementing her plan. Others may need to reassess at different intervals—weekly, monthly, semi-annually, or annually. No matter what timeline you create for accomplishing the projects necessary to launch and carry out your repotting plan, you'll need to address the sample tasks and issues covered in this chapter, as well as those that are unique to your situation.

Creating a Timeline: Three Milestones

We recommend creating a timeline with three phases: 6 months, 12 months, and 24 months. We've provided a template for these stages and sample tasks for each one in the *Repotting 101 Workbook* and in the Landscape Master Plan—Checklists and Timelines for Chapter 9, starting on page 207. You'll need to identify for yourself the specific tasks that you have to accomplish in order to reach your goals in each time frame. In doing so, you'll also be able to measure your progress. Keep in mind that repotting is an evolutionary process, as well as a revolutionary one. While it's true that you've decided to make a dramatic change, it won't occur overnight. Your new life will evolve and unfold over time.

No matter what kind of plan you've developed, our research shows that all repotters need to consider the following factors in developing their timeline: finances, relationships (with family members, friends, colleagues, and peers), home and lifestyle, logistics (having to take courses, set up an office, or arrange pet care), and intangibles (dealing with emotional issues and unforeseen outcomes).

We've chosen four repotting scenarios as prototypes and listed sample tasks that these types of repotters would need to accomplish in each time frame. Your own situation may be a variation on one of these, or it may be in its own class. Moreover, several of these groups have subcategories with their own examples. Our examples are just illustrations meant to assist you in thinking through your set of repotting tasks and timeline.

- **Category I** is for *a nonworking woman* who wants to join the workforce full- or part-time, or who decides to volunteer in order to bring more meaning into her life.

- **Category II** is for *a career woman* who wants to leave her current job in order to stop working entirely, work a reduced number of hours, volunteer, or do something new to find a more fulfilling life or who wants to start a new job in a new field.

- **Category III** is for *a woman who becomes an entrepreneur* for one of several reasons: She decides to leave a corporate job to have more control over her time and life; she wants to run a home-based business for family reasons; she's motivated to start her own company because of the independence it offers and the prospect of financial rewards; or she's a retiree who wants to fill her leisure time with a challenging venture rather than merely occupying her time with activities she doesn't find meaningful.

- **Category IV** is for *a woman who pursues enrichment activities,* such as obtaining an advanced degree in a subject of interest or training for a new skill or interest.

In the *Repotting 101 Workbook* or in the Landscape Master Plan for Chapter 9 (page 207), you'll find sample timelines showing 6-, 12-, and 24-month milestones that serve as logical checkpoints along the route of your repotting journey. These are the general guidelines, regardless of your situation:

- The first six months is the start-up phase. This break-in period encompasses getting organized, discovering your capabilities and limits and those of the people around you, setting up the foundation and structure of your plan, and finally launching it.

- The one-year point is the time when you should be refining your master plan. In this period, the goal is to be on your way, making necessary adjustments to the various aspects of your strategy as you move forward and pausing periodically to assess your progress.

- The two-year marker is when we suggest that you look back in order to look forward. By this time, you should have a good sense of whether the change you've made is bringing you the fulfillment you desire and is workable in your daily life, and whether you want to keep moving in the direction you've chosen.

These markers are suggestions only. We recognize that your repotting process may involve a wide variety of circumstances that cause you to move up the dates of your milestones or push them back. Unexpected opportunities or obstacles may arise, for when you change your status quo, you create a new state of disequilibrium in which you'll have to make constant adjustments. Try to be patient. Gardeners are accustomed to waiting for the end of winter, for saplings to grow into trees, and for seeds to mature into blooming plants. Repotters need to be patient, too.

Category I, Nonworking Woman Moving to a Full- or Part-time Job or Volunteer Position

This section examines the experience of nonworking women who repot, entering the workforce for one of several reasons. The first group includes women who have stayed at home to raise a family and haven't had the time or opportunity to work outside the home or pursue a volunteer interest full-time. A variation on this scenario is women who reenter the workforce after a number of years "off-ramp," a period in which they take a break from their former careers. Or, it could be an older retiree who decides to return to work. An estimated seven million previously retired people are now back at work or are looking for jobs. Nearly one-quarter of all people from the ages of 65 to 74 hold jobs, according to the Bureau of Labor Statistics.

The second group is women who are married and have spent the majority of their married life actively supporting their husband's endeavors but not working themselves. While they may have pursued some interests of their own during this time, they're now motivated to focus seriously on a new venture by joining the workforce or volunteering in order to fulfill their own desires.

The third type of nonworking woman is facing a change point in her life, such as divorce or the death of a spouse, that requires her to enter the workforce to support herself.

The checklists for Category I women are a little different depending on whether or not their plans involve a move to a full- or part-time position. Use our workbook or look at the Landscape Master Plan (page 207), where you'll find the checkpoints for both situations.

Pat's Story

Pat, a nonworking mother of three boys, had to grapple with joining the workforce full-time as the result of divorce. She had a law degree but hadn't worked in the past 15 years because she'd been at home raising her family. The upheaval in her marital situation forced her to plan for a new life and identity. To enhance and update her legal skills, she researched areas of the law that were growing fast and took classes in these fields. Having made the decision to join a firm so that she could support herself and her children, she spent six months networking extensively with friends and contacts in all areas of her life—including school, neighborhood, and church communities.

Thanks to a referral and recommendation from a parent at her children's school, Pat obtained a position at a local law firm. The time and effort involved in making the transition from being a stay-at-home mother to a full-time professional was difficult. She had to be very focused and goal-oriented in this journey because for her, repotting was a necessity and a matter of survival. Even though she had the luxury of an advanced degree, she still had to work her way through the turmoil and adjustments relating to this major change in her life.

Pat had to approach her timeline logistics with military precision. She created an entirely new schedule for her children that included all their activities and after-school care, as well as incorporating backup plans to cover possible illnesses and coverage during their school vacations. Her best-laid plans were frequently complicated by her uncooperative former spouse. She also faced financial challenges—start-up costs relating to her new role as the sole provider for her family—that required her budget to include phased payments for tuition and other expenses, which she had to negotiate with the school and her bank.

She also had to deal with the impact this significant disruption had on her children. Knowing that they were going to miss her in the role of a cookie-baking, always-available mom and daily chauffeur, Pat held several meetings with them to discuss the upcoming changes in their lifestyle. Although she didn't write out the new procedures, these sessions gave everyone an opportunity to express their feelings and provide input.

In the two years following her decision to reenter the workforce, Pat has made numerous adjustments and faced her fear factor. After transplanting herself into her full-time job as a lawyer, she has grown in many ways. She was worried that she might not be able to pull this off—that the kids would suffer, and she wouldn't be able to perform on the job. In her case, the biggest challenge in dealing with her timeline was overcoming the emotional intangibles of her repotting. By giving these concerns as much weight as the logistical, financial, and family factors, Pat ensured a successful transplant.

Variation on Category I: Nonworking Woman Choosing Part-Time-Only Work, Volunteer, or Interest Pursuit

You may decide that working or volunteering part-time or developing a special interest or talent is your repotting goal. Some women we interviewed have followed this path because it was, in their judgment, all that their family and they could handle. Others have done this as a way of experimenting with the notion of pursuing something that made them feel fulfilled without totally upending their life or that of their family. While a number of these women moved on from the experimental stage to full repotting, a number of them chose to remain partial repotters. (Review Chapter 8 for a description of partial repotting.) Some of our interviewees became cause-oriented volunteers when an event in their own lives led them to do so. We call them "change-point volunteers," and one is described in the next story.

Refer to the checklists at 6, 12, and 24 months that are outlined in our *Workbook* and on page 207 of this book in the Landscape Master Plan. In the first six months, the two areas that require additional tasks—dealing with finances and relationships—are also outlined on page 215.

Shelly's Story

Shelly had devoted herself to autism since her second daughter was diagnosed with this disorder at the age of two. Shelly and her husband came together to find ways they could help their child. Initially, she had to deal emotionally with the diagnosis while caring for her daughter and her other children. Meanwhile, her husband served as the family's information gatherer, attending conferences on autism in his spare time.

Shelly gradually became involved in an autism organization as a way to find answers to help her child, and other children as well. In her first phase of working as a volunteer, she attended conferences and events organized by this group. Over time, she defined her own mission, deciding that she was dedicated to creating hope for her family and others and finding a cure. Realizing that the group she originally joined didn't address these goals to her satisfaction, Shelly and her husband researched until they found what they were looking for—an organization called Cure Autism Now (CAN).

Once she came to terms with the long-term nature of her daughter's autism and her own need to be proactive in a search for solutions, Shelly launched herself into a new phase of life. She moved from being a nonworking woman with a family problem to a dedicated autism activist. She's a major fund-raiser for research into a cure for autism. In this role, she supports legislative efforts to generate more funding and hosts fund-raising events, including serving as the co-chair of the Cure Autism Now "Walk Now" national fund-raising event.

Shelly's repotting timeline included a six-month experimental phase that helped her define her own goals and mission. At the one-year mark, she began to refine her plan by joining CAN—an organization that shared her goals—and began to hit her stride with respect to her niche: fund-raising. At the two-year mark, she'd taken a leadership position in CAN and is now looking ahead for new ways to generate support and funding for autism research.

Shelly and her husband's involvement and commitment to this cause has brought her family closer together and helped them deal with a difficult issue in an open and positive matter. This is a case where a repotter and her spouse took a team approach to a change point in their lives and found fulfillment in dedicating themselves to a cause.

Category II: Career Woman Becoming a Nonworking Woman, Downshifting to Part-Time Work, or Switching to a New Job in a New Field

This section will look at career women who decide to repot in one of three ways. The first type of career-woman repotter (Category II-A) works either because she enjoys the nature of her job or for financial reasons. She decides to repot by leaving her job to start a family, spend more time with her current family, or find fulfillment in volunteering or because she's reached a significant milestone. Many of our interviewees told us that their frenetic pace as career women generated an uneasy sense that time was passing and they might be missing out on an authentic and meaningful life. Leaving full-time work is a seismic shift and requires careful planning.

The second kind of career woman repotter, Category II-B, is one who cuts back on full-time work for family reasons, to pursue a volunteer opportunity, or to explore an identified passion. Her sense of fulfillment is realized by straddling both the working and nonworking worlds.

The third group, Category II-C, includes career women who repot from one career to an entirely new one, making a dramatic change in their search for fulfillment. We've interviewed several of a growing number of women who are leaving successful professions for something entirely different—a lawyer entering a seminary, for example. One young repotter became disenchanted with nursing and left it to become a writer. Sometimes, a woman repots from a full-time career to an entrepreneurial venture. (These businesswomen will be discussed later in this chapter.) The checklists for Categories II-A, II-B and II-C are in the *Repotting 101 Workbook* and also begin on page 216 of this book.

Jennifer's Story

Jennifer was a consummate career woman who'd worked for four different businesses in the high-tech field, culminating in starting a company and growing it into a successful initial public offering (IPO) that was traded on Wall Street. She'd always placed family second to work when it came to allocating her time, because of her determination to provide a secure financial future for her children. She promised her two children that she'd retire once she accomplished her financial goals.

At the age of 50, Jennifer did just that. She made a conscious decision to change from being a career-consumed woman to a mother focused on her two teenage children, her love of animals, and a desire to "do something of value for the earth." She didn't regret the time she'd spent in the business world, but working was never the definition of the essential life for her.

When she retired, Jennifer wanted to begin a second career in volunteerism and pursue her interest in animal welfare. But first she took a couple of years to focus on her family and build a new house. She also joined the boards of a few public companies during this time because of her need to stay focused and busy after leaving such a demanding world. Then she turned her attention and energy to finding the right cause that could help her discover meaning in her life beyond her career. Her goal was to pick an organization that she could not only give money to, but also get passionately involved with.

In the first six months, Jennifer extensively investigated the world of animal-welfare issues and nonprofit groups. She identified not one but two organizations that she could envision herself being involved with as both a funder and a full-time volunteer on a long-term basis. Both were eager to take advantage of her executive experience, and within a year, she'd joined both organizations.

Jennifer's biggest challenge in making a successful transition was coming to terms with her emotional needs. On the job, where she'd received daily feedback and reinforcement for her contributions and skills, she'd found her identity through her work. Out of the office, no one was telling her why she mattered, and as a result, she had to redefine her identity and her sense of personal value.

By switching worlds—from the corporate realm to family and philanthropy—she lost contact with some members of her professional network. As their lives diverged, Jennifer had to seek a new circle of friends who shared her new interests. She satisfied her desire to give back and met some of her intangible needs through volunteerism. At the five-year mark, she's confident that her redesigned life landscape plan is on track and is providing the benefits she sought for herself and her family. Her children often join her in animal-welfare work, and the three of them have more time to vacation together.

Category III: Woman Becoming an Entrepreneur

As we pointed out earlier in this book, women are choosing this repotting solution in record numbers. They're starting businesses at twice the rate of men—the number of women-owned businesses reached 10.6 million in 2004. Women made up about 40% of all small-business owners in the U.S. in 2006, according to the Center for Women's Business Research. They're choosing this route for several reasons. First, it gives them flexibility, independence, and control that are often missing in a corporate setting. Second, it offers the possibility of making more money than they might be able to make working for someone else. Third, it meets the goal that many repotters have expressed of owning and building something for themselves or for a succeeding generation.

Not every entrepreneurial venture requires a staff. Many women start out as the sole proprietor of their business for financial reasons or because they're testing the concept and don't want responsibility for employees. This can be a viable solution for young singles, married women with and without children, and retirees because of the flexibility it provides. According to a recent study by the Center for Women's Business Research, there are 5.4 million women-owned businesses with no employees that generate $167 billion in sales annually.

Other female entrepreneurs establish partnerships so that they can share responsibilities and cover for one another. Overall, women-owned businesses generate $2.46 trillion in sales and employ 19.1 million people. Clearly, this is a path that more and more repotters are choosing to follow.

The milestones and tasks for all categories of entrepreneurs are included in the *Repotting 101 Workbook* and in the Landscape Master Plan in this book, beginning on page 229. Some businesswomen, such as franchisees or those enrolled in entrepreneurial training programs, may have the benefit of timelines provided for them by outside entities. If you're working with this type of plan, be sure to add in the tasks that relate to family and intangibles, as these considerations may not be covered in materials provided to you by other sources.

Kianna's Story

Kianna got married and emigrated from Africa to the midwestern United States in 1993. Although she had a college degree and a strong interest in all things artistic, her husband expected her to devote her time to managing their home and caring for his extended family who lived in the area. After many years of fulfilling these expectations, she was frustrated and felt she needed to do something for herself.

Initially, Kianna's strategy was to reconnect with her artistic interests and talents by enrolling in art school part-time. This enabled her to continue to fulfill her role as homemaker. Eventually, she decided to get a full-time, entry-level job outside the home, which she located through Internet research. While working in this position, Kianna brought samples of textiles from her home country into the office to sell. Co-workers were enthusiastic about her product line and encouraged her to start her own import business. Her husband, however, remained opposed to her working outside the home in any manner.

In spite of her husband's opposition and her lack of funding or business skills, Kianna decided to proceed with starting a textile-import business. In the first six months of planning her repotting, while researching funding opportunities, she learned about a contest sponsored by the local chamber of commerce. First prize for the best business plan was a cash grant of $5,000.

Through her network, Kianna sought out a retired executive who helped her write the plan. She submitted it, won the contest, and used the prize money to hire M.B.A. interns from a local college to help her carry out her start-up tasks and create a marketing plan for her new business.

At the one-year mark, Kianna was open for business but realized that she needed to supplement her entrepreneurial skills with additional training and add staff by tapping into her network. She enrolled in a course at a local women's business center to help her refine her plan, solve some start-up problems, and move to the next phase.

Along the road to repotting from a stay-at-home woman to an entrepreneur, Kianna changed her entire life landscape plan. She divorced her husband, changed her appearance to look more professional, took courses to add to her skills, and adopted an independent mindset that gave her confidence and a fresh outlook on her future. Today, she has a new network of friends, her business is thriving, and Kianna is feeling fulfilled!

Beth and Carol's Story

Beth, a married mother of two young children, quit her job due to a lack of flexible hours, which had been negatively impacting her family. Having watched both her parents start businesses on their own, she understood the advantages that an entrepreneurial venture could offer her. At the same time, she felt that having a partner would allow her to share responsibilities and financing and give her backup when it was needed. Because starting from scratch would have been too demanding, Beth researched franchising opportunities, hoping to start what she called a "business in a box." After identifying what she wanted, she found a partner, Carol, to share in the initial investment and become a co-owner.

Carol hadn't worked for 15 years while raising two teenage daughters. She was attracted by Beth's description of the business and had the necessary money to invest. What she didn't realize was that even a "business in a box" required a major commitment of her own time and effort in the start-up phase.

Carol didn't hold a family meeting and create a "family constitution" outlining the new responsibilities and commitments required of her teen daughters and spouse.

As a result, three months into the venture, she was faced with a rebellious family who wanted their life to return to the prebusiness state. To try to satisfy them, she cut back on work, leaving her partner to handle the bulk of the responsibilities. At that point, Beth's 70-hour workweek left her no time for her young children. Something had to give.

After months of negotiation, Beth realized that the partnership wasn't viable. She bought Carol out of the business and took on a new role as sole proprietor. She solved the time crunch by hiring and training highly capable staff to take on the duties of her former partner. At the one-year mark, she was doing so well that she was able to propose a second store to her franchise owner, and that plan has now been approved. Beth's success derived from her ability to recognize problems, address them, and find workable solutions.

Category IV: Woman Repotting for Enrichment

Women aren't just repotting to and from the working world. Many are motivated by a strong need for a sense of enrichment, which can be derived from a variety of sources. For some, education in and of itself offers the mental reward and challenge that brings meaning into their lives. Their learning process can take many forms; occur in different settings; and provide opportunities for meeting, enjoying, and networking with new friends. Enrichment repotters find fulfillment by exploring new subjects, acquiring new skills, rediscovering long-lost interests or passions, or expanding their horizons through travel and other kinds of new experiences.

Please refer to your *Repotting 101 Workbook* or page 237

in this book for this group's checklists in the Landscape Master Plan. You may also wish to refer back to the timelines for Category I repotters for additional guidance.

Lolo's Story

Lolo had grown up in Europe and studied art in Berlin before the beginning of the Second World War. After she came to the United States, she married, had children, and assisted her husband with his medical career. Having been a nurse during the war, she was able to build on that experience to become a scientific researcher in her husband's company. While raising her family, she began to teach children's art classes as a way to reconnect with her earlier passion.

By chance, a friend gave Lolo a piece of fiber-optic cable and suggested she create something with it. She began to experiment with sculpture using this medium and was fascinated with the process and her creations. She decided to turn this new pursuit into a full-time avocation and potential career. With the goal of having her own show, she created ten pieces, using a friend's basement as her studio. With her former training in art as a foundation, Lolo taught herself how to meld fiber optics and plastic to develop her own original sculptures. At the one-year mark, she was ready to launch herself as a sculptor in the public arena. Sculpture became and remained the central focus of her life for the next 30 years.

Lolo's immersion in this field didn't culminate with her commercial success as a sculptor. When she turned 70, she looked back on the fulfillment she'd received from this pursuit and wanted to share it with others. As she said, "If it brought me so much pleasure, I figured it might be able to do the same for others, especially the aging."

This led Lolo on her next repotting journey—the founding of a nonprofit organization dedicated to providing art classes for seniors with dementia and Alzheimer's. The organization, called Arts for the Aging, has grown from 2 to 50 centers in the Washington, D.C., metropolitan area. Now 90 years old, Lolo continues to repot, looking for ways to connect seniors with animals, another passion of hers.

> **Personal Gardening Tip:** Successful repotting requires that you create a customized timeline that reflects your individual set of circumstances, values, and goals. Attention to detail and a staged launch are critical to creating a workable plan.

Remember to refer to all the sample checklists and timelines for each category of repotter in your *Repotting 101 Workbook* or the Landscape Master Plan section of this book, which begins on page 207. Developing a specific strategy for putting your ideas into practice is the key repotting step for finalizing your plan to redesign your life.

Chapter Ten

Rules for Repotting

Many gardeners have benefited from the principles developed by Christopher Lloyd, gardener and writer extraordinaire, whose plant knowledge and horticultural insight have inspired people around the world. His ground rules also make up many of the concepts that provide the framework for gardeners and are derived from his own experiences and lessons learned in designing and planting a garden.

With a master landscape plan in hand, a woman can move from empty beds in spring to a glorious blooming garden by summer's end. Her goals may include coloring her landscape with the plants she wants, making her garden a unique reflection of her personality, and designing an environment that will flourish and last. To push the horticultural boundaries, a gardener knows she has to stay focused and involved. Along the way to bringing her vision to fruition, a successful gardener is guided by specific ground rules.

The first nine chapters of this book have given you some tools—exercises and lessons learned from other repotters—to help you design your own life landscape. As you launch your plan, you also need a set of ground rules to serve as the guiding principles for your repotting process.

We recognize that not every concept we've outlined will work for everyone and that you may even disagree with some of our ideas, but that's okay. Our goal is to stimulate, challenge, and energize you to start your journey. Just engaging in this process will help you hone your own opinions and create something that works for you. As garden writer Graham Rice said in his profile of Christopher Lloyd, ". . . gardening is as much about thinking about what you're doing, and what you've done, as it is about actually doing it."

As you embark on this experiment—and we call it that because repotters must enter new territory in order to change their lives—you need to have two things with you. The first, of course, is the repotting life landscape plan that you've developed as you've read the first nine chapters of this book. The second, contained in this chapter, is the essential list of rules for repotting that will serve as your crib sheet, providing guidance, inspiration, and validation as you actually repot. Whether you're a beginner, graduate, or veteran repotter, these rules will be a handy reference on your journey. You can use them as your handbook on your way to finding a redesigned life that's more fulfilling for you.

Rule 1: Change Your Mind-set— You Need a New Outlook to Repot

We've devoted more space to Rule 1 than to Rules 2 through 9 because it's the foundation upon which the other guidelines rest. Throughout this book, we've encouraged you to examine your outlook on a number of issues; we've also said that adopting a new perspective is the critical first step in repotting. This is important because no matter how well crafted your new life landscape plan looks on paper, successful implementation is totally dependent upon developing a new mental attitude.

One woman told us that after her husband of 32 years left her, she had to completely change her thinking in order to survive the trauma in her life. Her reeducation process allowed her to think about her future in a new way. Instead of withdrawing from the world, this repotter went back to her former career as a teacher and is now fully engaged in that profession. For you to transplant yourself successfully, you'll need to adopt new mind-sets in at least four areas: time, risk, engagement, and well-being.

Time: Slow Down; It's Not Happening

As you'll recall from Chapter 2, changing your time mind-set requires discipline and a new way of looking at your schedule. There are two pillars that support your new outlook, and the first is an imperative: Slow down! As long as you're running frantically through your daily maze, you'll have little chance of gaining the perspective you need to create the life you want. Vivian, a 38-year-old mother of three who was a full-time insurance adjustor, was never able to grab a moment for reflection because she allowed the rest of her life to spin out of control. To change, she needed to acknowledge that she had to take back control of her time and stop living a fast-forward life.

The second pillar of your new time mind-set is to learn a new term: "not happening." Adopting this attitude means underscheduling your day instead of overbooking it. Your schedule is in your hands. Start each morning by making a proactive decision about what you want to accomplish. This may mean listing only two things on your to-do list instead of eight.

Your new outlook also includes the ability to "deschedule." This means removing from your to-do list any activities that you know are nonessential. Then you need to create a new category called "not happening." These are the things that your gut tells you just can't be part of your day—the cost to you is too great!

An article in *The New York Times* discussed how many women and men are now choosing the "not happening" solution. The interesting part is how grateful both parties are when an event is cancelled, providing the individuals with the extra time they so desperately need and want but have been unable to create for themselves. Remember, the purpose of descheduling or weeding out your schedule is to create pockets of time for thinking and imagining how you want to live your life.

No Boundaries: Open Your
Mind and Take the Risk

One of the defining trends of this decade is women's willingness to push their limits, stretch themselves, and go beyond the expected. They've made the choice to open their minds to new possibilities, set goals that challenge themselves, and take the risks they need to grow and change. As repotters strive to explore new frontiers in their lives, their approach demands an open mind. Nothing is precluded; all is open for examination. This mentality requires courage and the ability to look beyond the old parameters and constraints, such as age, income, education, family status, tradition, or ethnicity. These are no longer considered insurmountable obstacles by modern women. They're being swept aside by the belief that there are no boundaries that can't be overcome if the desire and motivation are strong enough.

Embracing a risk outlook means being willing to live with vulnerability and uncertainty while trying something that's potentially beyond your capabilities. As we mentioned in Chapter 5, today's news is full of reports about female adventurers, whether they're in the sports arena or the corporate world. The repotters we interviewed all shared a common willingness to leave the comfort of the familiar, face the unknown, and set aside their fears. Transplanting yourself into a new life landscape means leaving your old pot or flower bed behind for a fresh growth environment. Having a "no boundaries" mind-set means giving up the comfort of old rituals, getting past your fear of failure, and finding a new identity in the context of a changed world.

Commit: Be Fully Engaged

A commitment mind-set is the foundation for redesigning your life. It provides the mental focus you need to stay on the repotting path and eliminate distractions that will take you away from your goal. Being fully engaged provides fuel that stimulates and energizes you for the work involved in redesigning your life landscape plan. Your metamorphosis depends upon your ability to concentrate your attention, laserlike, on the repotting tasks required to reach your goal.

In today's society, where many people expect instant gratification, easy solutions to difficult situations, and someone else to give them the answers to life's problems, repotters have learned one thing the hard way: There's no such thing as "repotting for dummies." Our interviewees told us that they had to be fully engaged in their own repotting process. This mind-set enabled them to create their own road map.

As you repot, adopt an immersion lifestyle. Whatever you choose to undertake, plunge in with total dedication. Your energy and drive may be directed at building a new career, volunteering, or pursuing a new hobby. But make your total commitment to repotting a given.

Self-Care: Tend to Your Own Well-Being

Think of yourself as a repotter in training. You need a self-care mind-set to ensure that you're equipped mentally, physically, and spiritually to undertake the steps necessary to achieve your redesigned life. Repotters have told us that bringing their own health and well-being to the forefront of their daily concerns is crucial because it fosters a positive outlook. Women gain confidence, stamina, and energy when they're in tune with their physical, mental, and spiritual selves. When these components are in alignment, they're "good to go" on their repotting mission.

As the gatekeepers of family health, many women extend their caretaking concerns to their spouse, children, friends, and even pets—and sometimes they put themselves last. Making your own well-being a priority is key. You, like other successful repotters, need to decide to take charge of your own health. You're at the center of all the issues surrounding you on a daily basis—your own health matrix.

Rule 2: Edit Your Life—Less Is More

Women are editing their lives on a daily basis, discarding what doesn't work and streamlining their worlds on every level. Closet consultants, life coaches, home organizers, and a raft of media offering tips on living simply are reflections of people's growing desire for clarity and order in an affluent, technology-driven society. While all these services are helpful, they provide only superficial assistance. The most important editing task is to commit to making room for meaning and fulfillment.

How do you start to pare down? We addressed the time issue in an earlier chapter and in the discussion of Rule 1. But this editing process ranges from reassessing how you schedule your day to what you buy or don't to how you can create a personal time oasis for reflecting and planning to repot. With a cluttered mind, you can't think clearly, much less redesign your life. Many repotters told us that they chose to forgo money, prestige, and everything that accompanies them in order to change their lives and have more time to pursue the thing that gave meaning to their days, whether it was family, horses, pottery, or travel.

Rule 3: Free Your Mindscape— Cultivate Your Imagination

If you've read Chapters 1 through 9 and done the exercises provided, you've immersed yourself in the details of creating a new life landscape plan. Those are tangible results. The intangible ingredient in the process is your imagination. To repot, you need to let your mind run free to entertain untested concepts. Repotters need to unleash their creative side in order to envision a new future for themselves. Actress Patricia Neal's daughter, Ophelia Dahl, commented in a *New York Times* profile that her father taught her how important the imagination is "as a guide, as a prop, [and] as a companion." She added, "He taught us that you'll never be truly alone if you have a great imagination. It enables you to empathize, to imagine yourself in someone else's position."

When one of our repotters left the profession she'd worked in for the past 15 years, she interviewed numerous friends and family members about what she should do next. She was determined to keep an open mind to any and all suggestions, and visualized herself in a wide variety of new roles. To do so, she had to tap into an ability that had been dormant since her childhood. Only after she opened the gates to her imagination could she benefit from the flow of new ideas from herself and her network. She went from corporate lawyer to pastry chef and told us that the change is providing the fulfillment she was seeking.

Rule 4: It's <u>Your</u> Landscape—
Be Proactive—Only You Can Change It!

It's an old adage that you reap what you sow. For repotters to achieve a successful transplant, they need to stop planning and start digging. As you navigate through the changing terrain of your life, flexibility is essential. Just as plants that survive are those that can adapt, you, too, must be flexible and versatile in your approach.

Each step in the repotting journey will present you with choices. The ability to respond, take detours when necessary, incorporate alternatives, and follow Plan B is essential if you're going to achieve a successful outcome.

Mastering life on the go requires mental and physical agility. One woman told us that she had to learn to be proactive in making her own choices. Repotters can't allow circumstances or outside influences to dictate their own decision making. Empowerment and growth come from facing issues head-on, running through your mental checklist, and finding your own solutions. Since you're your own life landscape designer, only you can make the final decisions about what will bloom and grow in your garden. Be poised to move forward!

Rule 5: Balance Is Bunk—
Learn to Live in a State of Disequilibrium

Achieving balance on a day-to-day basis is unrealistic because our lives are in a constant state of flux. While it may be possible over the long-term to bring different aspects of your life into harmony, the goal of having everything in balance all at once remains out of reach. Nevertheless, many women are still chasing this unrealistic goal, creating feelings of anxiety and failure and a sense of incompleteness. If you're consumed with the pursuit of balance, you won't have the time or energy to focus on what you need to do to redesign your life.

Women who are contemplating repotting their lives need to shift their views from seeking balance to learning to live with disequilibrium. This state is generated, in part, by the technology revolution that has put us all on call 24/7. The information avalanche that we experience affects our decision making on a daily basis, making it critical that we think and function in a new way. Constantly shifting circumstances cause repotters to have to keep alternatives open rather than invest themselves in single-path decisions. Get used to this, because as we look toward the future, it's likely to be a permanent condition in our lives.

Repotters need to look around for new avenues of growth even when their life situations seem to be devoid of opportunities. In these circumstances, we say: Don't allow yourself to be buffeted by constant change. Blossom where you're planted. Dig deep to discover the hidden flower garden in your life—don't dwell on the idea that your personal landscape is barren.

Lois, for example, has spent all her time focusing on family issues: her husband's business, her teenage children's lives, and the needs of an aging parent who lives in another city. She spends her day reacting to e-mails from her husband, calls from her parent, and messages regarding her children's school activities. All the while, her goal is to get everything in balance so that she can do what she really wants to: volunteer and make a difference.

But this is never going to happen unless Lois moves beyond the balancing act and looks at the philanthropic opportunities close at hand. Once she concentrates on her goal of volunteering and starts to cultivate a flower bed for it in her life, she'll be able to move toward her goal of helping others outside her family and being more fulfilled. Her new focus and the example she sets by helping others may also benefit her loved ones.

Rule 6: Find Your Authentic Self—Write Your Own Story

Women today are asking themselves: *Why put off being who I really want to be?* We don't have the luxury of living a "practice" life. This new mind-set is driving their search for their authentic selves. The motivation is often the psychic and emotional rewards of new pursuits, whether career oriented or not. As a repotter embarking on the search to find the "new me," you need to take the following steps:

1. Assess your current life.

2. Find what matters most to you and tailor your lifestyle to incorporate as much of it as you can.

3. Decide how much time you can afford to allocate to your area of interest in light of your family and financial situations.

4. Research your interest—things may have changed since you first discovered it.

Once repotters have made the decision to redesign their lives, identify the values they cherish, and make them part of a more meaningful lifestyle, they're ready to create their new life landscape plan. This book was designed to help you write your own Repotting 101 curriculum. As you launch the transplant plan of your life, you'll be creating a life that's customized for you.

Carla did just that. Always an animal lover, she wanted to spend less time on her career and more with her horse. She cut back on her clients to reduce her work hours, moved her office to her country home, and used technology to facilitate her new working arrangements. She took up dressage, enjoying the challenges inherent in this sport, and made a new network of friends. As she ages, Carla, a single woman, is aware that connecting with her horse fulfills her basic need for a bond with a living creature. She has customized her lifestyle to reflect her authentic self.

Rule 7: Go Beyond Yourself—Tap into Your Networks

Throughout this book, we've said that only *you* can repot yourself. That said, the good news is that you don't have to do so alone. You're surrounded by a variety of networks of family members, friends, and colleagues who may be able to give you feedback, advice, and emotional support along the way. A Duke University study found that a quarter of Americans say they have no one in whom they can confide. For repotters, obtaining feedback and input is an essential component of the process. We urge you to seek out and tap into your networks, no matter how difficult it may be, and, if necessary, find new communities to connect with.

One repotter made a concerted effort to tap into numerous networks before initiating her transplant. As a single career woman, she could draw on her base of work colleagues and her parents, as well as friends she'd made recently or whom she'd known since childhood. She consulted every single person in these networks, listened to their ideas, filtered the information, and selected the ideas that most interested her.

Married women with children have other avenues for networking, such as neighbors and parents from their children's schools and sports teams. Still others can draw on their church, local community organizations, hobby groups, and school. Another way to connect, especially if you live in a remote area, is to participate in online communities, such as chat rooms, that reflect your interests.

Just as gardeners rely on a variety of service providers to support their efforts, repotters need to draw on outside communities to help them create their new life landscape plan. One of the beauties of connecting with people is the potential for the help to go both ways: As you benefit from the advice of others, you may find that you're helping someone else along the way. Among the many blessings of repotting are the social relationships you build through networking along your repotting journey.

Rule 8: Learn for Life—Expand Your Knowledge, Expand Your Options

Ongoing learning is pivotal for women in every life stage. Whether you're a young single woman, a married baby boomer, or a retired senior, you need mental nutrients and vitamins to stimulate new thinking. The process can take many forms and occurs in a variety of venues. From pursuing an advanced degree to joining a book club to returning to campus to complete an interrupted degree program, women are adding to their skills portfolios throughout their lives. As they anticipate creating new identities for themselves, they engage in the learning process to ensure that they'll be prepared for their future endeavors.

Repotters seeking self-enrichment can benefit from lifelong learning in two ways: It facilitates reaching their specific repotting goal, and also helps them regenerate themselves through growth in the learning environment. One of our interviewees who's a successful entrepreneur decided to take painting and French classes to expand her horizons and explore those interests to determine if they were going to become repotting destinations. Although neither pursuit became her goal, the classes in and of themselves provided her with enjoyment, mental stimulation from learning something new, and respite from the demands of her entrepreneurial venture.

To repot, you need to keep this formula in mind: Learning equals stimulation, which fosters new growth and change—and acquiring knowledge and skills can happen at any age, in any situation.

Rule 9: Experiment—Embrace Trial and Error

A key tenet of repotting is that experimentation is a valuable tool. You need to probe the unknown to find new passions and paths to pursue. Trial and error are your friends; don't be afraid to test your ideas in real-life situations. Whether you succeed or fail, you'll still benefit from the lessons learned in the process of trying something unfamiliar. Until you plant a sample bed in your own personal garden, you won't know for sure if the conditions are right for growth. If they're not, you can always rip it out and start again. Life is full of choices that end up on the compost pile.

If your experiment works, however, you're poised for the next phase: becoming fully engaged in your repotting journey. Partial repotters who use the experimental stage to test their goals and concepts may go no further, as we discussed in Chapter 8. But full-blown repotters plant seedlings as an experiment, too, and learn from how they grow in order to implement their entire plan to redesign their lives. One woman focused on her own fitness to such an extent that she decided to try training others. In the course of establishing a personal one-on-one training business, she determined that her financial needs couldn't be met in this way. Although her experiment failed on one level, she gained a fit body, a new set of friends, and a new habit of self-discipline to apply to her next repotting journey.

Rule 10: Create a Legacy—Landscape for Longevity

Repotters, like gardeners, are motivated to create a landscape that will flourish and last. They know that there are no shortcuts; the process of growth is ongoing. A lovely, mature garden can take up to ten years to come to fruition. Similarly, establishing and living a redesigned life also requires an effort over time. In the process of changing your own environment, you may create something of value to pass on to others. Many of our interviewees repotted for their own benefit but also wanted to leave something of lasting value as a legacy.

Today's fast-forward lifestyles have created a deep need to stop, take stock, and gain a sense of place and heritage. Women have always played a key role in creating and maintaining traditions and preserving the family heritage—they're keepers of the family flame, creating tangible records and milestones for themselves and their loved ones. Repotting can fill the need that many women have to bequeath their values and the example of living a meaningful life to those they care for.

One such woman is Allyn, who left Hollywood after 20 years as a successful movie producer to focus on creating a family. For her, this meant adopting a child. Her goal as a single woman was to share herself and create a legacy. She moved to Idaho to pursue a new lifestyle centered on raising her son and enjoying the outdoors. Although she's deferred her career for the time being, she knows that at some point she'll return to the movie business she's always loved. For now, she's happy being a mother and has immersed herself in all her son's activities.

Sometimes *legacy* means passing down your values and work ethic to your child, and then sharing an experience with them. That's the case with Ann and Tiffany. Ann worked in several entrepreneurial ventures before opening her own real-estate brokerage firm. Her daughter, Tiffany, started her own career in event planning, moved into educational services, and later decided to join her mother in real estate. The mother-daughter team has started Hamilton Group Realty, where they've shared the challenges and rewards of working together to create a lasting legacy.

Once you've repotted successfully (and we hope this book has been the catalyst for you to redesign your life), you need to think about developing long-term maintenance rituals for your new life landscape. Some gardeners make it a morning or evening ritual to survey their plants, even if it's only for five or ten minutes. Repotters need to spend time taking stock of their progress on a regular basis as well. Keep your revised Personal Garden Calendar handy and review the Personal Gardening Tips periodically.

A New You!

Congratulations! You've joined the repotting movement. You're one of the lucky women who now understands more about herself, has opened new vistas, made new friends, and reaped the benefits of participating in a journey of self-discovery. No matter what you've done—or will do in the future—with your redesigned life landscape plan, we hope the journey you're taking will provide you with stimulation and the self-confidence to become a new you!

As you repot, you may need to remind yourself quickly of the **Ten Rules for Repotters.** As a handy reference tool, here they are all together:

Rule 1: Change Your Mind-Set—You Need a New Outlook to Repot

Rule 2: Edit Your Life—Less Is More

Rule 3: Free Your Mindscape—Cultivate Your Imagination

Rule 4:   It's *Your* Landscape—Be Proactive—
Only You Can Change It!

Rule 5:   Balance Is Bunk—Learn to Live in
a State of Disequilibrium

Rule 6:   Find Your Authentic Self—Write Your
Own Story

Rule 7:   Go Beyond Yourself—Tap into Your
Networks

Rule 8:   Learn for Life—Expand Your Knowledge,
Expand Your Options

Rule 9:   Experiment—Embrace Trial and Error

Rule 10: Create a Legacy—Landscape for
Longevity

Remember, there's no failure in the repotting process—life, like gardening, can be an endlessly joyful process. The thrill of finding something new and interesting to replace tired and wilted plants in your life's garden is valuable in and of itself. The art of reinventing your life is never finished.

APPENDIX

Landscape Master Plan

Checklists and Timelines for Chapter 9

Category I, Nonworking Woman
Moving into a Full-Time Position

Six-Month Checkpoints:
Get Started, Set Up, and Launch

1. Logistics: Identify issues and find solutions.

- *Identify any educational requirements for the job you desire and pursue them.* Sign up for and take any appropriate tests (such as the GRE). Enroll for any needed classes or online study and campus-based degree programs.

- *Perform your job search.* Use the Internet to hunt. Write and distribute your résumé. Make follow-up calls and do correspondence. Schedule interviews.

- *Attend to home management issues.* Upgrade and install home office equipment if necessary. Determine whether you want to delegate chores such as housecleaning, grocery shopping, and home maintenance to someone in your household or if you prefer to outsource them.

- *Assess how to handle your caretaking responsibilities.* Determine how you'll fulfill your obligations to your children, older parents, and pets (outsourcing some or most of their care).

- *Decide how to handle errands.* Determine whether you'll outsource errands from car inspection to dry cleaning, and figure out the scheduling.

- *Determine your personal logistics.* Figure out your plans for creating a work wardrobe, dealing with transportation needs, and eating lunch (or dinner) once you've committed to being away from home all day.

- *Locate new service sources near your new job.* Find the nearest and most convenient bank, doctor, pharmacy, dry cleaner, school, and so on.

- *Consider your job-related learning curve.* Do networking, research, and reading as necessary to assess what your learning curve will be.

2. Finances: Create a new budget.

- *Budget for logistical problems that you can no longer handle.* For example, you may have to pay a dog walker. If you can no longer participate in the school car pool, you may need to pay someone else to drive your children.

- *Budget for any new job- or education-related expenses.* These might include new housing and clothing, child care, taxes, tuition, travel, and extra food expenses (grocery delivery, takeout, restaurants, and so on).

- *Create a financial plan.* Consider whether you'll need a loan to start up a new business or pay tuition. Create a spending plan for your income after expenses, factoring in your new job-related costs. If you'll generate extra money, decide whether you'll save it, invest it, or use it to pay off debts.

3. Relationships: Consult family, friends, and your other networks about the changes you'll be making regarding your home and personal life.

- *Hold a family meeting to create a new family constitution*—a document written in consultation with your family members that provides a protocol for the future covering of responsibilities, schedules, and so on.

  — Meet with your spouse and children to get their commitment to your plan and goal.

  — Address family- and personal-scheduling issues to make time for yourself and others. For instance, if you and your husband decide that he'll attend an after-school activity, you'll need to schedule time for your own exercise or entertainment, and so on.

— Divide up responsibilities among family members. These might include household chores, car pools for school and extracurricular activities, homework, and so on.

— Revise the rules for how parents and children will contact each other. For example, you might decide that the children will check in with you by calling you at the office when they arrive home after school.

— Review your plans for emergencies, such as if there's an accident at home.

— Make any other needed adjustments. You might decide to have your spouse or children prepare breakfast or lunch or get a commitment from extended family members to supervise or act as emergency contacts.

- *If you're single, consult members of your support network.* Identify and discuss your plan with family members, friends, and others to tap into your support system.

4. Intangibles: Address other important issues related to your repotting.

- *Take stock of your emotional issues resulting from your repotting.* Consider whether you'll be able to cope emotionally with the changes, for example.

- *Assess the impact of your new job on the attitudes of your family or friends.*

- *Think about how you'll adjust emotionally and physically to your new schedule.* Consider how you'll handle sleep deprivation, overwork, low energy, and so on.

- *Consider age issues.* Think about whether you'll be able to adjust to the habits, office rules, technological demands, and lexicon in a workplace where you're considerably older or younger than your co-workers. If you're going back to school, consider whether you'll be comfortable attending classes with people younger than you are.

- *Confront any fears and insecurities.* Address fears of failure, overcome insecurities about your performance on your new job or your ability to handle schoolwork, and so on. Seek counseling if necssary.

Category I, Nonworking Woman Moving into a Full-Time Position

12-Month Checkpoints: Refine Your Master Plan

1. Logistics: Identify problems and adjust strategies where it's necessary to do so.

- *Consider your job plan.* Have you met your professional goals, or your objectives for getting the education you need for the switch? Do you feel you've at least made progress? If you have a job now, do you feel comfortable with your work? Is there room for advancement? If the answer to any of the above is *No*, refer to Plan B—your backup plan.

- *Consider your education.* Is your change strategy working for you? Do you need to consider getting more education? If you're taking classes, are the courses meeting your needs, are the subjects of interest, and is the workload tolerable?

- *Consider other logistics.* Review all of your other logistical arrangements and fine-tune them according to your needs, paying special attention to caretaking arrangements to ensure that your children, parents, or pets aren't showing signs of stress, even if everything else in your plan is working smoothly.

2. Finances: Consider your income and expenses.

- *Take another look at your budget.* Is it realistic or does it need revising?

- *Think about your salary requirements.* Determine whether the expenses, stress, and changes associated with your new job (or your potential new job) are worth the benefits.

3. Relationships: Assess whether your plan meshes with your family's needs (or, if you're single, assess whether you can get help or input from your network).

- *Hold another family meeting or, if you're single, meet with members of your support network.* Review your family members' issues, responsibilities, and schedules. Consider how your new job or your pursuit of further education is impacting everyone in your family or network and whether you need to adjust something.

4. Intangibles

- *Set aside time to consider your own well-being.* How are you doing, emotionally and physically? Have you taken on too much? Is your plan absorbing all of your time? Do you need to readjust your schedule to accommodate the needs of your family and yourself? Are you working so hard to succeed that you haven't created enough time for attending to your emotional, physical, and spiritual needs?

Category I, Nonworking Woman
Moving into a Full-Time Position

24-Month Checkpoints:
Look Back to Look Forward

1. Look back.

- *Review the last two years and confirm that you're on the right path.*

- *Decide whether you want your involvement in your chosen field to expand, stay the same, or be reduced.*

If you're a partial repotter, you may want to go full-steam ahead with pursuing school, a career, or volunteer opportunity.

2. Look forward.

- *Plan your next move.* Based upon what's happened in the last two years, decide whether you want to take more courses, pursue a promotion, or accept a position of greater responsibility in your volunteer organization.

3. Reconsider.

- *Think about repotting again.* Taking into consideration what's happened in the last two years, determine whether you want to repot again. You may even want to switch directions and become a serial repotter as a result of changing life circumstances or just for the challenge of it. If this is what you decide to do, refer back to the first six months of this section, or perhaps look at Categories III and IV (beginning on page 229). You might decide that what you really want to do is start your own business or spend more time pursuing a hobby.

Category I Variation, Nonworking Woman to Part-Time-Only Work, Volunteer or Interest Pursuit

6-Month Checkpoints: Additional

1. Finances

- *Review your budget.* Often, much of the salary for part-time work is eaten up by the expenses associated with the job. If you take a part-time volunteer position, remember that you won't be making money but instead will be spending it on such things as transportation, food, child care, and so on. When pursuing an interest, you won't make money, but may spend it on taking classes or on expenditures related to the endeavor (such as buying scuba equipment or supplies for scrapbooks). Of course, you may find ways to offset these expenses, such as the sale of pottery you make, carpooling with others, and so on. Be sure you've planned accordingly to absorb these expenses.

2. Relationships

- *Hold a family meeting or, if you're single, meet with members of your support network.* Family members may be resentful about the increase in expenses, the disruption to their schedules, or other conflicts of interest if you take a part-time job or volunteer position or you devote more time to pursuing an interest. If so, these feelings need to be discussed. If you're single, see if your network can provide input or assistance.

Category II-A, Career Woman Who
Becomes a Nonworking Woman

6-Month Checkpoints:
Get Started, Set Up, and Launch

1. Logistics

- *Handle issues related to resigning from your job.* Determine when you'll give notice. Cash out (or roll over) investment plans and vacation pay. Transfer your health insurance. Close out work-related projects (for example, you may need to train your replacement).

- *Handle home management, caretaking, and personal logistics.* Review your procedures and establish new ones as needed.

2. Finances

- *Create a new budget or financial plan in light of your loss of income.*

3. Relationships

- *Hold a family meeting or, if you're single, meet with members of your support network.* Review the new circumstances and determine how the family is going to respond. If you're single, check in with your support network to see if they can offer input and assistance.

4. Intangibles

- *Address the emotional impact of the changes you're making.* Think about whether you're comfortable with your loss of status, title, salary, colleagues, and the personal satisfaction you derive from a career and professional networks.

- *Expand your circle of friends and interests.*

- *Deal with any feelings of guilt.* Get in touch with and work through any guilt you may be feeling about your loss of income or not fulfilling your own or others' expectations of yourself.

Category II-A, Career Woman
Who Becomes a Nonworking Woman

12-Month Checkpoints:
Refine Your Master Plan

1. Logistics

- *Review and make adjustments to your household and caretaking arrangements as needed.*

2. Finances

- *Reevaluate your budget.* Ask yourself whether the sacrifices associated with giving up your income are too great.

3. Relationships

- *Hold a family meeting or, if you're single, meet with members of your support network.* Take the family's temperature: Find out how your plan is working for them and how they feel about your not working at this juncture. If you're single, consult your network regarding whether they can continue to provide input and assistance as needed.

4. Intangibles

- *Review your situation.* Do you like what you're doing, and are you feeling more fulfilled?

- *Review your own activities.* Do these outside events provide enough stimulation and challenge? Have you preserved enough personal time for yourself and for reflection on your repotting process?

Category II-A, Career Woman Who Becomes a Nonworking Woman

24-Month Checkpoints:
Look Back to Look Forward

Look back.

Review the last two years. Is your off-ramp life— one you've led after leaving your job—pro- the fulfillment you were seeking when you repotted? Is this solution beneficial not only for you but for those around you? Do you miss the challenges associated with your former career enough to want to rethink your decision?

2. Look forward.

- *Consider rejoining the workforce.* If you still hanker for the challenge of the career world at this point, you may want to consider going "on-ramp"—rejoining the workforce—in a part- or full-time position. There may be financial or other reasons for you to resume working in some capacity. The solution for some repotters has been starting an entrepreneurial venture from home—"mom inventors" are a perfect example of this. Some women become franchisees to skip the start-up requirements of a new business venture. (See the section on entrepreneurs, beginning on page 229.)

- *Hold a family meeting or, if you're single, meet with members of your support network.* Take stock of how things are going and obtain input on any new ideas you may have for your repotting plan.

*Category II-B, Career Woman Who Goes Part-Time
in Work in Order to Volunteer or Pursue an Interest*

**6-Month Checkpoints:
Get Started, Set Up, and Launch**

1. Logistics

- *Negotiate with your employer about a new schedule
  and set of responsibilities to allow you to downshift.*

- *Negotiate a revised work package (such as vacation,
  health benefits, and salary).*

- *Review and establish new home-management
  solutions (housekeeping, child care, and so on) as
  needed.*

- *Take classes and join groups that can help you
  pursue your interests or desire to do volunteer work.*
  Join committees, boards, and membership organizations to determine the best fit with your
  volunteering goal. Take classes to help you find
  your niche.

2. Finances

- *Create a new budget and financial plan in light of
  your reduced income stream.*

3. Relationships

- *Hold a family meeting or, if you're single, meet with
  members of your support network.* Determine the

impact of your reduced work on the family, and see what changes and revisions need to be made to responsibilities and schedules. If you're single, consult your network to see if they're willing to provide input and assistance.

4. Intangibles

- *Assess the emotional impact of your reduced workload.* Consider how you feel about your title, salary, and relationship with your colleagues. Think about whether you're comfortable with how others view you and how you feel about your new life and schedule.

- *Devise a strategy for meeting new friends and finding fresh interests.*

- *Deal with any feelings of guilt.* Get in touch with and work through any guilt you may be feeling about your loss of income or not fulfilling your own or others' expectations of yourself.

Category II-B, Career Woman Who Goes Part-Time in Work in Order to Volunteer or Pursue an Interest

12-Month Checkpoints:
Refine the Master Plan

1. Logistics

- *Assess your household management and caretaking needs.* Review and make adjustments as needed to the child-care and house-management arrangements established in the first six months.

2. Finances

- *Reevaluate your budget.* Review expenses, including the loss of income associated with having reduced your work and dedicated more hours to volunteering. Do the benefits outweigh the costs?

3. Relationships

- *Hold a family meeting or, if you're single, meet with members of your network.* Allow family members to give input on how your change is working for them emotionally and practically. Discuss with them or supportive friends whether you need to adjust responsibilities and schedules in order to get their assistance or support.

4. Intangibles

- *Review your situation.* Do you like what you're doing? Do you feel fulfilled? At this point, you should have a clear sense of whether you made the right decision about repotting.

- *Review your leisure activities and amount of personal time.* Do your outside commitments provide enough stimulation and challenge for you? Have you preserved enough personal time for yourself and for reflection on your repotting process?

Category II-B, Career Woman Who Goes Part-Time in Work in Order to Volunteer or Pursue an Interest

24-Month Checkpoints:
Look Back to Look Forward

1. Look back.

- *Determine if you met your repotting goal in the last two years.* Decide if the part-time work schedule works for you and your family and whether the work itself is fulfilling. Are you experiencing reduced stress and an increased sense of meaning in your life?

2. Look forward.

- *If you decide that you want to continue in your part-time status but change the nature of your job,* review the steps outlined in Category I, Nonworking Woman Moving to Full-time Position, to start your search.

- *If you determine that a better solution would be to stop working altogether,* refer to Category II-A, Career Woman Becoming a Nonworking Woman, and the logistics section checklist for resigning from your job and handling the related issues.

- *If you decide to resume full-time work,* you'll need to decide if you want to return to your previous career or start a new one. Review Chapters 6 and 7 to think through all your options.

- *Look ahead to the next three to five years.* Think through what you want your life to be like. If the initial reasons that prompted you to repot will change in that time frame, you should be thinking ahead to how your repotting will fit with these shifting circumstances. For instance, if your toddlers may all begin school in the next few years, would you consider going back to work full-time?

Category II-C, Career Woman
Switching to a New Job in a New Field

6-Month Checkpoints:
Get Started, Set Up, and Launch

1. Logistics

- *Resign from your current job.*

- *Handle issues related to resigning from your job.* Determine when you'll give notice. Will you resign from your job before looking for a new one? Cash out (or roll over) investment plans and vacation pay. Transfer your health insurance. Close out work-related projects (for example, you may need to train your replacement).

- *Find your new job.* Determine if you need further education or new skills. Research careers online and through your network. Attend meetings related to your field of interest and join professional groups if necessary. Revamp your résumé. Contact employers. Go on interviews and follow up afterward.

- *Address the learning curve of your new job.* Schedule meetings with co-workers, read background materials, and take classes as appropriate.

- *If you'll be in a new locale (neighborhood or city), find solutions for logistical issues.* Consider where you'll live, bank, eat, park, and so on.

- *Review the 6-month checklist for logistics provided in Category I, Nonworking Woman Moving to Full-Time Work.* Make any adjustments that are necessary.

2. Finances

- *Review and revise your current budget and financial plan.* Take into account your revised income projections. If your new job pays less than your old one did, what adjustments do you need to make? If your new source of income depends on commissions, have you set aside enough money to take you through dry spells?

3. Relationships

- *Meet with your family or members of your network.* Discuss your new venture and obtain feedback from them. Revise schedules as needed and consider whether you need to reassign responsibilities.

4. Intangibles

- *Establish your professional credibility and your personal self-confidence to overcome any fear of failure when starting your new job.*

- *Deal with any feelings of guilt.* Come to terms with the amount of time you're investing in learning and mastering your new job and the effect on your family and friends.

- *Find your emotional comfort level in your new position as you develop relationships with new colleagues.*

Category II-C, Career Woman
Switching to a New Job in a New Field

12-Month Checkpoints:
Refine the Master Plan

1. Logistics

- *Assess your caretaking and household-management needs.* Review how you're handling household-management, child-care, and other caretaking responsibilities.

- *Consider what you want to do next on your job and start developing a strategy to do it.* You may need to research more about how you can achieve a promotion, or you might have to get further education to improve or maintain your skills.

2. Finances

- *Reassess your budget.* Customize your financial plan to reflect your new position and revised fiscal goals. Determine if your new job will require a longer and more costly commute, a revamped wardrobe, travel that would necessitate extra child-care expenses, or anything else that could have an impact on your budget.

3. Relationships

- *Review and assess the impact your new job is having on your family and friends.* Discuss with them whether you need to adjust schedules or reassign responsibilities.

4. Intangibles

- *Assess your feelings.* Do you like what you're doing, and are you feeling fulfilled?

- *Consider whether you have enough personal time.* Have you preserved enough personal time to allow yourself to reflect on your repotting process and assess all the ways it's impacting you and those around you?

Category II-C, Career Woman
Switching to a New Job in a New Field

24-Month Checkpoints:
Look Forward to Look Back

1. Look back.

- *Does your new job arena provide the fulfillment you're looking for?*

- *During the last two years, have you felt that your life has changed for the better?*

2. Look forward.

- *If you don't feel that you made the right decision, you have several options.* If your financial situation allows it, you can stop working and take time to consider alternative plans, new careers, or other options. You can seek another position in the same field. A third option would be to engage in some form of enrichment to enhance your credentials in your new field so that you can advance your career or obtain a different job.

Category III, Woman Becoming an Entrepreneur

6-Month Checkpoints:
Get Started, Set Up, and Launch

1. Logistics

- *Prepare a business plan.* Make sure to define your niche and target your customers.

- *Prepare a marketing plan.* This should include strategies for networking, advertising, and doing mailings, as well as joining any local or national professional groups that could be of help to you.

- *Determine how and when you'll announce the opening of your business.*

- *Set up your business.* Create your home office (equipment, wiring, phones, technology, letterhead, business cards, and so on), obtain any business-related software you'll need, and handle other requirements as they arise. If your company isn't based in your home, you'll need to locate and lease space and possibly renovate it.

- *Fulfill legal and tax requirements and obtain certifications.* Arrange for any licenses, corporate registrations, insurance, permits, health inspections, and other requirements specific to your particular business.

- *Identify tasks you can't or don't want to do and determine how to outsource them.* Consider whether you'll need a receptionist, accountant, marketing expert, bookkeeper, order fulfillment service, and so on. Think about whether you want to have part-time and self-employed help, part-time workers, or full-time staff. If you're considering hiring anyone, talk to an accountant and a lawyer about your legal and tax obligations (such as creating W-2 forms, providing benefits for employees, and so on).

- *Identify and hire an attorney, if necessary.* You may need professional assistance to draw up leases, contracts, and papers for incorporating or establishing a partnership agreement and to provide other business legal services.

- *Create an application system—standard or online— for hiring staff.* If your new business will require you to employ others, for greater efficiency, you may want to set up an online application process that will allow you to weed out applicants who don't meet your needs, as well as help you develop relevant human-resources materials.

- *Create a board of advisers to provide guidance, expertise, and credibility when getting started.* This may consist of a mentor, a colleague, an expert in the field, a leader in the business community, an investor, and any other individuals whose names or credentials enhance your venture.

230

- *Identify appropriate modes of delivery for goods and services.* Depending upon your type of business, you'll need to determine how to deliver your products (such as by Express Mail, truck, air, local delivery, van, or messenger) or your services.

- *Choose appropriate office and work hours.* Take into account your working style and customers' and family's needs.

- *If you're in a partnership, establish rules for working together.* Decide upon procedures relating to work responsibilities, finances, and communication.

2. Finances

- *Prepare a detailed budget.* Make cash-flow projections, especially with respect to the timing of the first income stream. Decide if loans or supplemental cash infusions will be needed to tide you over until you make enough money to pay yourself.

- *Establish accounts and procedures for handling your business finances.* Set up bank accounts and online payment access, codify your accounting procedures, and so on.

- *Set up a tax entity, if necessary.* You may need to obtain state and federal tax ID numbers and fill out and submit any necessary related tax forms. An accountant will be able to help you with this.

- *Obtain financing, if necessary.* You may be able to get loans from banks, government programs (such as the Small Business Administration), family members, friends, or local community programs. Have a lawyer draw up an agreement to cover terms of loans from family members or friends. Establish lines of credit and obtain investors if it's appropriate to do so.

- *Review your business budget if it will impact on your family.* You need to allow your family to have input if you're taking money for your business from family savings.

3. Relationships

- *Meet with your family or members of your network to discuss your plan.* Review schedules, discuss how to handle responsibilities, and create a backup plan to deal with unforeseen events and emergencies.

- *If you're creating a business partnership, discuss nonbusiness issues* that might impact the venture (such as communication, work ethic, and work styles), as well as business issues (such as travel and cash contributions).

- *If you've hired staff, meet with your employees* to clarify your business mission, establish open lines of communications, and lay out your plan for the first six months.

- *Identify entrepreneurial support networks and mentors.* You can research this through the Internet as well as community and other organizations.

4. Intangibles

- *Define what you mean by "success" and how you'll measure it* in the first six months of your venture.

- *Review your schedule* to be sure it includes time for family (or friends) and personal commitments.

- *Acknowledge the possibility of failure and feelings of being overworked and overwhelmed.* Consider how you'll handle these feelings.

Category III, Woman Becoming an Entrepreneur

12-Month Checkpoints:
Refine Your Master Plan

1. Logistics

- *Undertake a comprehensive business review to assess your progress.*

- *Take steps to solve key issues.* These might include cold-calling potential clients, doing e-mail blasts and mailings to solicit customers, and broadening your network.

- *Meet with suppliers, vendors, and service providers.* Review procedures and discuss any issues that need to be addressed.

- *Make any necessary changes to your business plan and operation.* You may need to hire or fire staff, increase or decrease the amount of office space you have, buy or lease equipment, and so on.

- *Review outsourcing and "insourcing" arrangements to determine if changes are necessary.* You may need to handle more things in-house for financial reasons. Conversely, if your business is booming, you may need to subcontract some tasks to outside professionals.

- *Meet with your board of advisers as appropriate.* Your board can give you advice on opportunities for expansion, new products, sources of additional financing, and so on.

2. Finances

- *Review financial progress and needs.* Invest in expansion or cut back on expenses, identify and obtain new sources of cash, pay down loans, create financial incentives for employees, review compensation packages, and so on.

- *Evaluate your personal reimbursement.* Consider whether you need to draw a higher or lower salary and whether you need to cut down or even increase your various types of expenses.

- *Review your tax-payment schedule and filings.* Make sure that you're in compliance with the law.

- *Pay any yearly premiums.* These may include insurance, registration and certification fees, and memberships.

3. Relationships

- *Meet with your family or, if you're single, your network.* Discuss the impact your business endeavor has had on your relationship dynamic. Make adjustments to schedules and reassess responsibilities as needed.

- *If you're in a partnership, evaluate it.* Is it working or not? If not, is now the time to make a change?

4. Intangibles

- *Evaluate the intangibles of your plan and progress so far.* In spite of ups and downs, has your first year in business been fulfilling and energizing? Is your repotted life meeting your needs and goals? Have you achieved "success" at the one-year mark—according to your definition?

- *Consider the effects of your plan on your dependents.* Do you see signs of stress in your spouse, children, pets, or friends? Take steps to address any issues.

- *Consider the effects of your plan on you.* Are you overtired, depressed, lethargic or fatigued, or feeling guilty? If so, address these feelings.

Category III, Woman Becoming an Entrepreneur

24-Month Checkpoints:
Look Back to Look Forward

1. Look back.

- *Review your original business plan.* Was it realistic and does it need revision?

- *Assess where you are and whether you've met the goals you set.* Do you feel that you've been moving in the right direction toward your repotting goal over the last two years? If not, why not?

2. Look forward.

- *Create a revised business plan if necessary.* You may want to expand your existing business beyond its original concept, add new services, narrow its scope, refine certain goods and services, and so on.

- *Consider the sellout option.* You might want to sell your business but retain a limited role in it to allow yourself more flexibility. You might also want to sell it entirely to get a cash infusion so that you can pursue another business, because your financial goals haven't been met, or to take advantage of an unforeseen opportunity that presents itself.

- *Evaluate your partnership from a financial perspective.* Consider whether you want to buy out your partner's share in the business in order to meet her needs or yours.

- *If you're a sole proprietor, consider adding a partner to share the load or for a new source of cash investment.*

Category IV, Woman Repotting for Enrichment

6-Month Checkpoints:
Get Started, Set Up, and Launch

1. Logistics

- *Get started.* Enroll in enrichment classes or training sessions, begin traveling, or engage in other kinds of new pursuits.

- *Make changes in your home environment.* Set aside space dedicated to your enrichment activity (such as a study area, hobby spot, equipment storage unit, and so on).

- *Attend to caretaking responsibilities.* Arrange and schedule care for children, parents, and pets in order to create time to pursue your own enrichment.

- *Address personal logistics.* Buy, rent, or borrow necessary clothing or equipment you'll need for your new pursuit.

- *Determine and obtain any special licenses or insurance related to your endeavor.* This might include procuring insurance for scuba diving or horseback riding, buying a fishing license, and so on.

2. Finances

- *Create a realistic budget for your pursuit.* Decide how you'll pay for your enrichment activities.

3. Relationships

- *Meet with your family or members of your support network.* Describe and discuss your enrichment goals.

- *If appropriate, consult with others pursuing your new endeavor.* You may be able to share costs, responsibilities, transportation, and so on.

4. Intangibles

- *Is your choice creating the sense of fulfillment you seek?*

- *Do you need to make minor modifications in your enrichment plan?*

Category IV, Woman Repotting for Enrichment

12-Month Checkpoints:
Refine the Master Plan

1. Logistics

- *Make modifications to your enrichment program.* Expand or contract the number of hours you're devoting to classes, training sessions, studio time, trips, and the like. Investigate group versus one-on-one training, whether one location is more convenient than another, and so on.

- *Enroll in a degree program, more intensive training, or higher-level classes if you'd like to pursue your area of interest even further.*

- *Make adjustments at home.* Review and reassign responsibilities for caretaking and other duties and change schedules as needed.

2. Finances

- *Make budget adjustments.* Consider whether you want to expand or contract your enrichment program and how that will affect your finances.

3. Relationships

- *Meet with friends and family.* Determine if anyone wants to join you in your endeavor.

- *Assess the impact of your program on your relationships.* Identify any negative effects your enrichment program is having on your family or
  friends and problem solve if necessary.

4. Intangibles

- *Consider whether your enrichment pursuit is meeting your repotting goals.*

Category IV, Woman Repotting for Enrichment

24-Month Checkpoints:
Look Back to Look Forward

1. Look back.

- *Evaluate your level of satisfaction with your repotting process in the last two years.*

2. Look forward.

- *Identify new ways to explore your enrichment pursuit.* For example, are the classes you're taking
  at the right level for you? Do you have the right
  teacher?

- *Identify the appropriate next step in your enrichment process.* Make plans and pursue the next step. For example, you might move from being a student into being a teacher, from practicing an instrument alone to playing with a quartet, from taking community-center classes to enrolling in a degree program, or from taking group hikes to making self-guided trips.

Resources for Chapters 1–9

Note: The resource information included in this Appendix was correct at the time of publication.

Chapter 1

For help with time management:
www.balancetime.com/index.php
www.mindtools.com/page5.html

It's Hard to Make a Difference When You Can't Find Your Keys: The Seven Step Path to Becoming Truly Organized, by Marilyn Paul, Ph.D. (New York: Penguin, 2003)

Time Efficiency Makeover: Own Your Time and Your Life by Conquering Procrastination, by Dorothy K. Breininger and Debby S. Bitticks (Deerfield Beach, Fla.: Health Communications, 2005)

Women Who Think Too Much: How to Break Free of Overthinking and Reclaim Your Life, by Susan Nolen-Hoeksema, Ph.D. (New York: Henry Holt and Company, 2003)

Chapter 2

For working moms and help with time management:
www.momsrefuge.com
www.jobsandmoms.com
www.womenforhire.com
www.jobsformoms.com
http://life.familyeducation.com/parenting/working-parents/34415.html

For babysitters:
    www.sittercity.com
    www.babysitters.com

For cleaners:
    www.cleaningassociation.com
    http://csia.org

For home-service contractors:
    www.angieslist.com
    www.servicemagic.com

For the best home services in New York City; Los Angeles; Chicago; Connecticut and Westchester, New York; Chicago; and southeast Florida:
    http://franklinreport.com

For electric contractors:
    http://necaconnection.com

For interior design:
    http://asid.org

For life management:
    www.derbyservice.com

Everything I Need to Know I Learned from Other Women, by B.J. Gallagher (York Beach, Maine: Conari Press, 2002)

Chapter 3

For health:
    www.webmd.com
    www.pslgroup.com/dg/medrefsites.htm (Provides links to national and international sites containing information on a wide range of health topics.)
    www.medlineplus.gov
    www.medscape.com/welcome
    www.patientlinx.com/index.cfm
    www.medicineonline.com
    www.mdlinx.com
    www.mayoclinic.com

For nutrition:
> www.mypyramid.gov
> www.dietitian.com
> www.frenchwomendontgetfat.com
> www.eatright.org/cps/rde/xchg/ada/hs.xsl/index.html
> www.ediets.com
> http://diets.aol.com
> http://nutrition.about.com

Intuitive Eating: A Revolutionary Program That Works, by Evelyn Tribole and Elyse Resch (New York: St. Martin's Press, 2003)

Ultrametabolism: The Simple Plan for Automatic Weight Loss, by Mark Hyman, M.D. (New York: Scribner, 2006)

The Shangri-La Diet, by Seth Roberts (New York: G. P. Putnam's Sons, 2006)

For spiritual guidance:
> www.beliefnet.com
> www.explorefaith.org
> www.google.com/Top/Society/Religion_and_Spirituality/
> http://worldprayers.com

Inner Peace for Busy Women: Balancing Work, Family, and Your Inner Life, by Joan Z. Borysenko, Ph.D. (Carlsbad, Calif.: Hay House, 2005)

I Know I'm in There Somewhere: A Woman's Guide to Finding Her Inner Voice and Living a Life of Authenticity, by Helene G. Brenner, Ph.D. (New York: Gotham Books, 2004)

Emotional Comfort: The Gift of Your Inner Guide, by Judith M. Davis, M.D. (Chicago: Wilder Press, Inc., 2005)

A Weekend to Change Your Life: Find Your Authentic Self After a Lifetime of Being All Things to All People, by Joan Anderson (New York: Broadway Books, 2006)

Happiness: A Guide to Developing Life's Most Important Skill, by Matthieu Ricard (Boston: Little, Brown & Co., 2006)

Seven Sins for a Life Worth Living, by Roger Housden (New York: Harmony Books, 2005)

For philanthropy:
>www.goodsearch.com
>http://philanthropy.com
>www.charitywatch.org
>www.volunteermatch.org
>www.volunteer.org.nz
>www.idealist.org

For sleep help and insomnia:
>www.nhlbi.nih.gov/health/public/sleep
>www.shuteye.com
>www.sleepfoundation.org

Power Sleep: The Revolutionary Program That Prepares Your Mind for Peak Performance, by James B. Maas, M.D. (New York: HarperCollins, 1998)

For help quitting smoking:
>www.FFSOnline.org
>www.quitnet.com
>www.anti-smoking.org

For stress:

Positive Energy: 10 Extraordinary Prescriptions for Transforming Fatigue, Stress, and Fear into Vibrance, Strength, and Love, by Judith Orloff, M.D. (New York: Three Rivers Press, 2005)

For depression:
>www.moodgym.anu.edu.au
>www.depression.com
>www.psychologyinfo.com/depression

For exercise:
>www.shape.com/getfit
>www.healthypeople.gov
>www.fitness.gov/fitness.htm

For care of aging parents:
>www.benefitscheckup.org
>www.alz.org/carefinder

The Merck Manual of Health and Aging: The Comprehensive Guide to the Changes and Challenges of Aging—for Older Adults and Those Who Care for and About Them, by Mark H. Beers (Ed.) (New York: Pocket Books, 2004)

How to Care for Aging Parents, by Virginia Morris (New York: Workman Publishing Co., 2004)

Chapter 4

For senior employment:
> **www.retireecareers.com**
> **www.jobbank.org**
> **www.yourencore.com**
> **www.seniorjobbank.com**
> **www.dinosaur-exchange.com**

For federal student-aid loans:
> **www.fafsa.ed.gov**

For senior job training and placement:
> **www.servicelocator.org**
> **www.experienceworks.org**
> **www.doleta.gov/seniors**

The Power Years: A User's Guide to the Rest of Your Life, by Ken Dychtwald and Daniel J. Kadlec (New York: John Wiley & Sons, 2005)

My Time: Making the Most of the Bonus Decades After 50, by Abigail Trafford (New York: Basic Books, 2004)

Inventing The Rest of Our Lives: Women in Second Adulthood, by Suzanne Braun Levine (New York: Viking Penguin, 2005)

Chapter 5

For outdoor adventure:
> **www.outwardbound.org**
> **www.adventuresports.com**
> **www.uoadventures.com**
> **www.nols.edu**

For fitness:
> **www.self.com/challenge**
> **www.justmove.org**

For help starting a running program:
www.runnersworld.com (use the "Smart Coach" tool on the home page)
www.usatf.org/routes

For triathletes:
www.triathlete.com
www.beginnertriathlete.com

For trying new things:

You Can Do It! The Merit Badge Handbook for Grown-up Girls, by Lauren Catuzzi Grandcolas (San Francisco: Chronicle Books, 2005)

Chapter 6

For finding your passion:

Live What You Love: Notes from an Unusual Life, by Robert Blanchard and Melinda Blanchard (New York: Sterling, 2005)

Satisfaction: The Science of Finding True Fulfillment, by Gregory Berns, M.D., Ph.D. (New York: Henry Holt and Co., 2005)

What Should I Do With My Life?, by Po Bronson (New York: Random House, 2002)

A Matter of Choice: 25 People Who Transformed Their Lives, edited by Joan Chatfield-Taylor (Emeryville, CA: Seal Press, 2004)

Change the Way You See Everything: Through Asset-based Thinking, by Kathryn D. Cramer and Hank Wasiak (Philadelphia: Running Press, 2006)

Flow: The Psychology of Optimal Experience, by Mihaly Csikzentmihalyi (New York: Harper Perennial, 1991)

Mindset: The New Psychology of Success, by Carol S. Dweck, Ph.D. (New York: Random House, 2006)

Inspiration: Your Ultimate Calling, by Dr. Wayne W. Dyer, Ph.D. (Carlsbad, Calif.: Hay House, 2006)

The Spark: Igniting the Creative Fire That Lives Within Us All, by Lyn Heward and John U. Bacon (New York: Currency, 2006)

The Happiness Hypothesis: Finding Modern Truth in Ancient Wisdom, by Jonathan Haidt (New York: Basic Books, 2004)

Cure for the Common Life: Living in Your Sweet Spot, by Max Lucado (Nashville: W. Publishing Group, 2006)

True to Yourself: Leading a Values-Based Business, by Mark Albion (San Francisco: Berrett-Koehler Publishers, 2006)

Chapter 7

For career:
> **www.careerbuilder.com**
> **www.career-intelligence.com**
> **www.womenforhire.com**
> **www.womensmedia.com**
> **www.simplyhired.com**
> **www.aftercollege.com**
> **www.weddles.com**
> **www.theladders.com**

What's Really Holding You Back?: Closing the Gap Between Where You Are and Where You Want to Be, by Valorie Burton (New York: Waterbrook Press, 2005)

The Other 90%: How to Unlock Your Vast Untapped Potential for Leadership and Life, by Robert K. Cooper (New York: Three Rivers Press, 2001)

Speaking Your Mind in 101 Difficult Situations, by Don Gabor (New York: Conversion Arts Media, 2005)

The Martha Rules: 10 Essentials for Achieving Success as You Start, Grow, or Manage a Business, by Martha Stewart (New York: Martha Stewart Living Omnimedia, 2005)

The Unofficial Guide to Starting a Small Business, by Marcia Layton Turner (New York: Hungry Minds, 1999)

Whoops! I'm in Business: A Crash Course in Business Basics, by Richard Stim and Lisa Guerin (Berkeley, CA: Nolo Press, 2005)

Leading from the Front: No-Excuse Leadership Tactics for Women, by Courtney Lynch and Angie Morgan (New York: McGraw-Hill, 2006)

The Human Side of High Performance: Empowering Yourself for the Future, by Steven B. Wiley (Dubuque, Iowa: Kendall/ Hunt Publishing, 1998)

100 Best Nonprofits to Work For, 2nd Edition, by Leslie Hamilton and Robert Tragert (Lawrenceville, New Jersey: Peterson's, 2000)

101 Best Home-Based Businesses for Women, 3rd Edition: Everything You Need to Know About Getting Started on the Road to Success (For Fun and Profit), by Priscilla Y. Huff (Roseville, Calif.: Prima Publishing, 2002)

Do What You Are: Discover the Perfect Career for You Through the Secrets of Personality Type, by Paul D. Tieger and Barbara Barron-Tieger (Boston: Little, Brown, & Co., 2001)

What Color is Your Parachute 2007?: A Practical Manual for Job-Hunters and Career-Changers, by Richard Nelson Bolles (Berkeley, CA: Ten Speed Press, 2006)

Midlife Crisis at 30: How the Stakes Have Changed for a New Generation—and What to Do About It, by Lia Macko and Kerry Rubin (New York: Plume, 2005)

For locating freelance work:
> **www.dice.com**
> **www.freelanceworkexchange.com**
> **www.hireweb.com**
> **www.guru.com**
> **www.sologig.com**
> **www.programmingbids.com**
> **www.hotjobs.com**
> **www.monster.com**
> **http://entrepreneur.com**
> **www.fiveoclockclub.com**

Weekend Entrepreneur: 101 Great Ways to Earn Extra Cash, by Michelle Anton and Jennifer Basye Sander (New York: Entrepreneur Press, 2006)

For life coaching:
    Cheryl Richardson: **www.cherylrichardson.com**

For career growth:
    www.myguidewire.com

For personality assessment:
    www.myersbriggs.org

For information on careers in criminal justice:
    Bureau of Justice Statistics: **www.ojp.usdoj.gov/bjs/**
    National Criminal Justice Reference Service: **www.ncjrs.gov/**
    U.S. Department of Justice: **www.usdoj.gov/**
    State level: **www.state.**[stateabbreviation]**.us** (for example,
    New Jersey's site is: **www.state.nj.us**)
    American Bar Association: **http://www.abanet.org/crimjust/
home.html**

For the Women's Business Center directory:
    www.repotting.com/WBC Directory.pdf

For the National Association of Women Business Owners directory:
    www.repotting.com/NAWBO LISTING.pdf
    www.nawbo.org/chapters/index.php (local chapters)

For the Hispanic Business Women's Alliance:
    www.hbwa.net

For the National Latina Business Women Association:
    www.nlbwa.com

For the Latina Leadership Network:
    www.latina-leadership-network.org

For the National Black Business Trade Association:
    www.nbbta.org

For the Minority Professional Network:
    www.minorityprofessionalnetwork.com

Chapter 8

For starting a new business:
    count-me-in.org
    makemineamillion.org
    ladieswholaunch.com
    womenbusinessresearch.org
    wellsfargo.com/biz/intentions/women_bus_svcs.jhtml

For information about funding a new business:
    angelcapitaleducation.org
    goldenseeds.com

For locating part-time employment:
    www.craigslist.com
    www.snagajob.com
    www.jobsearch.about.com/od/parttimejobs
    www.employmentguide.com

For locating a part-time volunteer opportunity:
    www.servenet.org
    www.hud.gov/volunteering/index.cfm

Chapter 9

For small-business questions:
    e-mail: **smalltalk@wsj.com**

To access "small talk" archives:
    http://www.startupjournal.com/columnists/smalltalk/

For entrepreneurship:
    www.franchisehandbook.com
    http://www.entrepreneur.com/ebay
    http://www.i-soldit.com

For résumé building and writing:
    www.jobweb.com/Resumes_Interviews
    www.jobdirection.com/features/tips.asp
    www.e-resume.net
    http://resume.monster.com
    www.vault.com

www.e-resume.us
www.resume-resource.com
http://owl.english.purdue edu/workshops/hypertext/ResumeW

Now What? 90 Days to a New Life Direction, by Laura Berman Fortgang (New York: Tarcher, 2005)

How Did I Get Here? Finding Your Way to Renewed Hope and Happiness When Life and Love Take Unexpected Turns, by Barbara DeAngelis (New York: St. Martin's Press, 2005)

Acknowledgments

First and foremost, we want to thank our husbands, Jim Holman and Stuart Pape. Their love, patience, and support were essential to us in writing this book.

To our children, Adams Holman and Hilary Shaw and Sam and Sarah Pape, we thank you for your feedback, your editorial comments, and your understanding during our strenuous writing schedule.

Without our agent, Jillian Manus, president of Manus & Associates Literary Agency, Palo Alto, California, this project would never have gotten off the ground. Not only did she serve as the catalyst for writing this book, but she also provided a wealth of inspiration and ideas about how to explore this subject. Her assistant, Dru Gregory, was always happy to help us in any way.

To Reid Tracy, president, Hay House, Inc., we're truly grateful to you for believing in our concept from the beginning, making a home at Hay House for this book, and all your support along the way.

To the wonderful Hay House team, many, many thanks: Jill Kramer, our editor and friend, and Jessica Vermooten, assistant editor, both of whose patience and wisdom carried us through from start to finish; Christy Salinas, Margarete Nielsen, Jeannie Liberati, and Jacqui

Clark for their many contributions; Roberta Grace and John Thompson for their efforts on our behalf; Cara Sammartino, our publicist; and Amy Gingery for her outstanding cover design.

To Lynda Carter, who graciously agreed to write the Foreword to this book: You immediately saw the connection between our topic and your own life and how this book could help so many other women.

Thanks also to Lila Fendrick, landscape architect and founder of Evergro Landscape, Chevy Chase, Maryland, for her valuable insights into the landscape design process, and ongoing guidance in connecting landscape gardening to the repotting process.

We are also grateful to Nancy Peske for her editorial assistance.

To Chris Boskin and Tina Frank, who have lent their creative support and contacts throughout the writing process: Thank you, dear friends!

We're deeply grateful to Donna Anderson, Sicklesmith Design, and Lee Anderson, Anderson Multimedia, for their invaluable assistance with our Website, **www. repotting.com**, and photography.

To Dr. James B. Maas: Thanks for your professional input as well as your encouragement in the writing process.

To our friends:

Diana's friends—Gigi, for her friendship and great listening skills while walking dogs; tennis friends—Daphne, Rosalie, Bonnie, Lee, and Suzanne for their patience on and off the court; and Karon, whose support, enthusiasm, and humor were invaluable.

Ginger's friends—Francesca, Karen, Laurie, Ellen, Ginny, and the Gal Pal Group—in gratitude for their beautiful hearts and their friendship, help, and kindness throughout this project.

We give special thanks for the efforts of our research assistants: Joanna Russo, for her organizational and technological support; Kate Wiley, for her public relations assistance; and Anna Carpenter, for her research assistance in the initial phase of our project.

To Fatima da Silva, we're so grateful for all the nourishment—tea and cookies—you provided as we wrote at the kitchen table.

As amateur gardeners, we know that input from a wide variety of sources is invaluable for making our gardens bloom. As writers, we've benefited from the contributions of family members, friends, colleagues, and women repotters in this effort. To all the women repotters who took the time to share their stories with us, we say thank you and congratulations! Your experiences have inspired us write this book and will serve to help others who want to join the repotting movement.

About the Authors

Diana Holman is an entrepreneur and well-known trends expert who speaks worldwide to corporate audiences on lifestyle trends. She cofounded WomanTrend, the first company to analyze and interpret trends created by and affecting female consumers. In this area, Diana has consulted for Fortune 500 companies, including Nike, Anheuser-Busch, Procter & Gamble, Estée Lauder, Lifetime Television, *USA Today*, Kimberly-Clark, Avon, and Coca-Cola, among many others. Diana was the editor of *WomanTrends,* the firm's quarterly newsletter, whose subscribers included CEOs of companies such as Bloomingdale's and Hershey's. Since selling WomanTrend in 2001, she has focused her efforts on marketing and trends consulting. *Repotting: 10 Steps for Redesigning Your Life* is the natural extension of her trends research and entrepreneurial endeavors.

Ginger Pape is a former Wall Street executive, and Washington-based corporate officer of a Fortune 100 company. She helped found both the Women's Business Center (WBC), which trains women to start and/or expand their own businesses, and the Susan G. Komen Breast Cancer Foundation "Race for the Cure" in Washington, D.C. As an entrepreneur, Ginger founded and ran two separate consulting businesses, representing such clients as the American Stock Exchange, Scripps League Newspapers, and the Susan G. Komen Breast Cancer Foundation. Over the last 15 years, she has advised women from all walks of life on their repotting process. Drawing on the accumulated stories of women she has helped, Ginger is now ready to share her repotting expertise in *Repotting: 10 Steps for Redesigning Your Life.*

Website: **www.repotting.com**

We hope you enjoyed this Hay House book.
If you'd like to receive a free catalog featuring additional
Hay House books and products, or if you'd like information
about the Hay Foundation, please contact:

Hay House, Inc.
P.O. Box 5100
Carlsbad, CA 92018-5100

(760) 431-7695 or **(800) 654-5126**
(760) 431-6948 (fax) or **(800) 650-5115 (fax)**
www.hayhouse.com® • **www.hayfoundation.org®**

Published and distributed in Australia by: Hay House Australia Pty. Ltd.,
18/36 Ralph St., Alexandria NSW 2015 • *Phone:* 612-9669-4299
Fax: 612-9669-4144 • www.hayhouse.com.au

Published and distributed in the United Kingdom by: Hay House UK, Ltd.,
292B Kensal Rd., London W10 5BE • *Phone:* 44-20-8962-1230
Fax: 44-20-8962-1239 • www.hayhouse.co.uk

Published and distributed in the Republic of South Africa by: Hay House SA
(Pty), Ltd., P.O. Box 990, Witkoppen 2068 • *Phone/Fax:* 27-11-706-6612
orders@psdprom.co.za

Published in India by: Hay House Publishers India, Muskaan Complex,
Plot No. 3, B-2, Vasant Kunj, New Delhi 110 070 • *Phone:* 91-11-4176-1620
Fax: 91-11-4176-1630 • www.hayhouseindia.co.in

Distributed in Canada by: Raincoast, 9050 Shaughnessy St., Vancouver, B.C.
V6P 6E5 • *Phone:* (604) 323-7100 • *Fax:* (604) 323-2600 • www.raincoast.com

Tune in to **HayHouseRadio.com®** for the best in inspirational
talk radio featuring top Hay House authors! And, sign up via the
Hay House USA Website to receive the Hay House online newsletter
and stay informed about what's going on with your favorite authors.
You'll receive bimonthly announcements about Discounts and Offers,
Special Events, Product Highlights, Free Excerpts, Giveaways, and more!
www.hayhouse.com®